Living
Together
Multi-Family Housing Today

Living Together

Multi-Family Housing Today

For Zonk

Published in Australia in 2007 by
The Images Publishing Group Pty Ltd
ABN 89 059 734 431
6 Bastow Place, Mulgrave, Victoria 3170, Australia
Tel: +61 3 9561 5544 Fax: +61 3 9561 4860
books@images.com.au
www.imagespublishing.com

The Images Publishing Group Reference Number: 706

National Library of Australia Cataloguing-in-Publication entry:

Crosbie, Michael J. (Michael James).
Living Together: Multi-family Housing Today

ISBN 1 86470 236 2

1. Apartment houses. 2. Architecture, Domestic – Designs and plans. 3. Community development, Urban. I. Title

728.314

Edited by Andrea Boekel

Designed by The Graphic Image Studio Pty Ltd. Mulgrave, Australia
www.tgis.com.au

Digital production by Splitting Image Colour Studio Pty Ltd, Australia
Printed by Sing Cheong Printing Co. Ltd. Hong Kong

Contents

Living Together in Harmony with Style by Michael J. Crosbie 6

Metro Hollywood Transit Village, Los Angeles, California, USA 10
Kanner Architects

Contemporaine, Chicago, Illinois, USA 16
Perkins + Will

Orange Grove Lofts, West Hollywood, California, USA 24
Pugh + Scarpa Architecture

Solaire, New York, New York, USA 30
Pelli Clarke Pelli Architects

1212 Euclid, Santa Monica, California, USA 34
David Forbes Hibbert, Architect

Radio City, Toronto, Ontario, Canada 40
architectsAlliance

Italian Gardens, San Jose, California, USA 46
Seidel Holzman

Folsom Dore, San Francisco, California, USA 52
David Baker + Partners

North Court, Boulder, Colorado, USA 56
Wolff Lyon Architects

Parent Avenue Lofts, Royal Oak, Michigan, USA 58
McIntosh Poris Associates

Waterloo Heights, Los Angeles, California, USA 64
Koning Eizenberg Architecture

Brownstones at Riverfront Park, Denver, Colorado, USA 68
Humphries Poli Architects

Bergamot Artist Lofts, Santa Monica, California, USA 74
Pugh + Scarpa Architecture

Esther Short Commons, Vancouver, Washington, USA 80
William Wilson Architects

Magnolia Row, West Oakland, California, USA 86
David Baker + Associates

Briar Hills, Omaha, Nebraska, USA 90
Randy Brown Architects

Harold Way, Los Angeles, California, USA 96
Koning Eizenberg Architecture

Douglas Meadows, Portland, Oregon, USA 104
Robertson, Merryman, Barnes Architects

Bentley-Massachusetts, Los Angeles, California, USA 106
Kanner Architects

18 Yorkville, Toronto, Ontario, Canada 112
architectsAlliance

Lenzen Square, San Jose, California, USA 116
David Baker + Partners

Main Street North, Boulder, Colorado, USA 118
Wolff Lyon Architects

San Pedro Commons, Colma, California, USA 122
Seidel Holzman

Wentworth Commons, Chicago, Illinois, USA 126
Harley Ellis Devereaux

Venice Beach Lofts, Venice, California, USA 132
Steven Ehrlich Architects

Rollins Square, Boston, Massachusetts, USA 138
CBT Architects

K Lofts, San Diego, California, USA 146
Jonathan Segal, Architect

Commerce Street Townhomes, Dallas, Texas, USA 152
Ron Wommack Architect

11th Avenue Townhomes, Escondido, California, USA 158
Studio E Architects

Box & One Lofts, Portland, Oregon, USA 164
Fletcher Farr Ayotte and Kevin Cavenaugh

8th and Howard Apartments, San Francisco, California, USA 168
David Baker + Partners

Rose/Knox Townhouses, Houston, Texas, USA 172
Donna Kacmar, Christopher Craig, Mary Ann Young

Loyola Village, San Francisco, California, USA 176
Seidel Holzman

Blake Street Flats, Denver, Colorado, USA 184
Humphries Poli Architects

Homesafe, San Jose, California, USA 188
Studio E Architects

Laconia Lofts, Boston, Massachusetts, USA 194
Hacin + Associates

Avenue Lofts, Fort Lauderdale, Florida, USA 198
Krupnick Studio

Tip Top Lofts, Toronto, Ontario, Canada 204
architectsAlliance

Colorado Court, Santa Monica, California, USA 208
Pugh Scarpa Kodama

Church Condominiums, Boston, Massachusetts, USA 212
R. Wendell Phillips and Associates

Fahrenheit, San Diego, California, USA 218
Studio E Design, Martinez Cutri (Executive Architect)

Index of Architects 222

Acknowledgments 224

Living Together in Harmony with Style

By Michael J. Crosbie

Multi-family housing is alive and well. Despite the fact that in North America the single-family home is exalted as the key ingredient of the "American Dream," the varieties and qualities of multi-family housing—where families and individuals of all stripes and shapes live close together—continue to grow.

Today there is greater emphasis in multi-family housing design on expressing individual identity. Many of the projects in this book are inventive in the ways that one's home within the collective is easily identified. In many cases this is accomplished by creating and celebrating a path from the street to the front door. For example, the North Court project uses pitched roof forms of different heights, porches, and front doors—all elements that people closely identify with an image of "home." This helps to make each unit recognizable from where one enters the North Court community and walks to his or her front door. Even in a relatively large project such as Wentworth Commons, which contains more than 50 affordable apartments, the mass of the building is articulated in vertical divisions of color, setback, and form that allow one to readily point to, say, the distinctive green bay in the middle and say to a friend, "that's where I live." The Blake Street Apartments also uses vibrant color to provide units with an individual character, as does the 8th and Howard Apartments with its colorful mural.

The 11th Avenue Townhomes likewise use color and other visual cues to identify individual units, even though the plans of all the units are identical. Designed for low-income renters, the design of 11th Avenue eliminates the stereotype of low-cost housing as anonymous and repetitive. The affirmation of the individual units, and the people who live in them, is achieved through sensitive design.

One of the strongest themes found in this collection of multi-family housing is sustainability. Many architects have embraced design that conserves natural resources, offers alternative fuel sources, and brings living into greater harmony with nature. Reusing old structures for new housing is one of the most sustainable approaches. For years, old factories and mills have been transformed into multi-family housing. Some of the more ingenious projects herein include The Tip Top Lofts, which turned a former warehouse and Art Deco landmark in Toronto into a chic new residence, with several new floors added on top. The reuse of a brick garage as new retail and community space for the new Folsom Dore project shows that a small structure can be reborn as part of a community. In this case, the new building nearly absorbs the old structure, revealing just its brick façade. Recycled buildings of another sort are seen in the K Lofts project, which reuses commercial strip buildings retrofitted for new multi-family housing. One of the most spectacular examples of reuse is the Church Condominiums project, where a Catholic church and rectory have been converted into multi-family housing. Decorative details of the old church are preserved to become unique features of the condo interiors.

Like other projects with a sustainable slant, Douglas Meadows uses energy conservation features and durable, low-maintenance materials to keep the life-cycle costs of this affordable housing development low over the long haul. The Achilles Heel of "affordable" housing has long been its higher living costs due to poor energy performance (resulting in higher utility and fuel bills) and inferior materials that need costly replacement. Douglas Meadows and projects like it demonstrate that one of the keys to affordability is sustainable design and construction.

The sustainable features in many projects are barely perceptible. However, architects are finding ways to make such elements as renewable energy technology more than just a "tack on." For example, photovoltaic installations are often placed on the roof with little fanfare, and in some cases there is an effort to conceal them. In the case of Colorado Court, the PV panels became a major part of the building's aesthetic expression. Portions of the five-story façade are covered with PV panels that not only generate part of Colorado Court's electricity, but also give it a bluish/silver aura.

Another aspect of designing with nature is finding ways to bring the outside into the building, and successful strategies can be seen in a number of projects located in benign climates. The Venice Lofts uses large glass garage doors in many of its living spaces, which open completely onto gardens and private patios. When closed, these glass walls still permit enjoyment of the natural world from inside. The same feature is used in the Orange Grove Lofts project, where the glass wall in a living room slides into the wall, opening the space to the outdoors. In some cases, making the line between inside and outside porous is an urban design strategy. In the Box & One Lofts, for example, the glass garage door in a first-floor bistro rolls up to allow passersby on the sidewalk to see inside, and permits restaurant patrons to partake in the street life just beyond the threshold. One story up, the glass roll-up door in an apartment brings in the bustle of the bistro and the street below.

The Box & One Lofts reflects another trend in multi-family housing: the combination of living and working places. Before modern zoning practices separated living and working spaces, it was common to find apartments where work also took place—within the unit itself or in more semi-public spaces nearby. Architects and planners now see the benefits of such arrangements to the life of the city, and municipalities are rewriting zoning laws or permitting variances to allow live/work arrangements.

An excellent example of this trend is seen in the Bergamot Artist Lofts. This development near an art center in Santa Monica, California, includes ground level studio/gallery spaces, with three levels of artist live/work lofts spaces above. The Laconia Lofts in Boston, Massachusetts, have a similar arrangement of studios and galleries on the ground floor, with artist lofts above. The loft interiors are bare bones canvases to encourage residents to create their own designs.

Many of these multi-family projects accentuate affordability, some taking advantage of government programs that encourage the design and construction of multi-family housing at or below the median income of the neighborhood. One of the most inventive affordable projects is the Rose/Knox Townhouses, affordable units built for a very special population: architects. Three former classmates, now all practicing architects, decided to build their own multi-family townhouse project as a way to lower their housing costs. This infill project uses low-cost materials rendered in inventive, artful ways to create efficiently designed units of 1600 square feet. The final construction cost of $50 per square foot proves that architects (particularly those motivated by savings for their own pocketbooks) can create well-designed and appointed housing.

Consider this volume a pattern book of contemporary multi-family housing solutions to a wide variety of design and construction challenges, to inspire more projects to meet the needs of living together in harmony with style.

Selected

Projects

Metro Hollywood
Transit Village

Los Angeles, California, USA

Kanner Architects

Metro Hollywood is a mixed-use development built above an MTA subway station at Hollywood Boulevard and Western Avenue. It is a mixed-use transit village that enables its residents to commute easily around the city on subway trains and buses. The project contains a 60-unit, low-income housing development with mostly two and three-bedroom apartments situated above a base of 10,000 square feet that includes retail space and a childcare center.

Metro Hollywood was designed to be a prototype with environmental, social, and aesthetic benefits. For instance, the building exceeds by 20 percent state codes regarding energy efficiency. The design integrates the project with the neighborhood by lining up the project's large courtyard with the existing courtyard of an adjacent housing project and by creating a greater open space between the projects. In addition to being a cost-effective project, it has a colorful, uplifting modernist design that is aesthetically compatible with the design features of the Metro rail station below.

The project's main challenge was maintaining schedule and budget. The building required an expedited permit process because it had to be built within a tight schedule dictated by state funding requirements for affordable housing. Tenants had to move in within a tight time period for tax credit purposes.

Hefty steel framing, required to support the project above the subway station, was costly and required creative solutions elsewhere to maintain budget and still deliver a visually dynamic design. One such solution was to reduce the number, size, and sound-attenuation performance of the windows, but place them strategically in vertical and horizontal patterns that managed the same effect of limiting noise from the street outside and trains underground. A further measure taken to stay within budget was to use painted plaster rather than more expensive materials to mimic the color pallet of the MTA station.

bottom Site plan shows subway entrance
opposite Colors were inspired by subway station

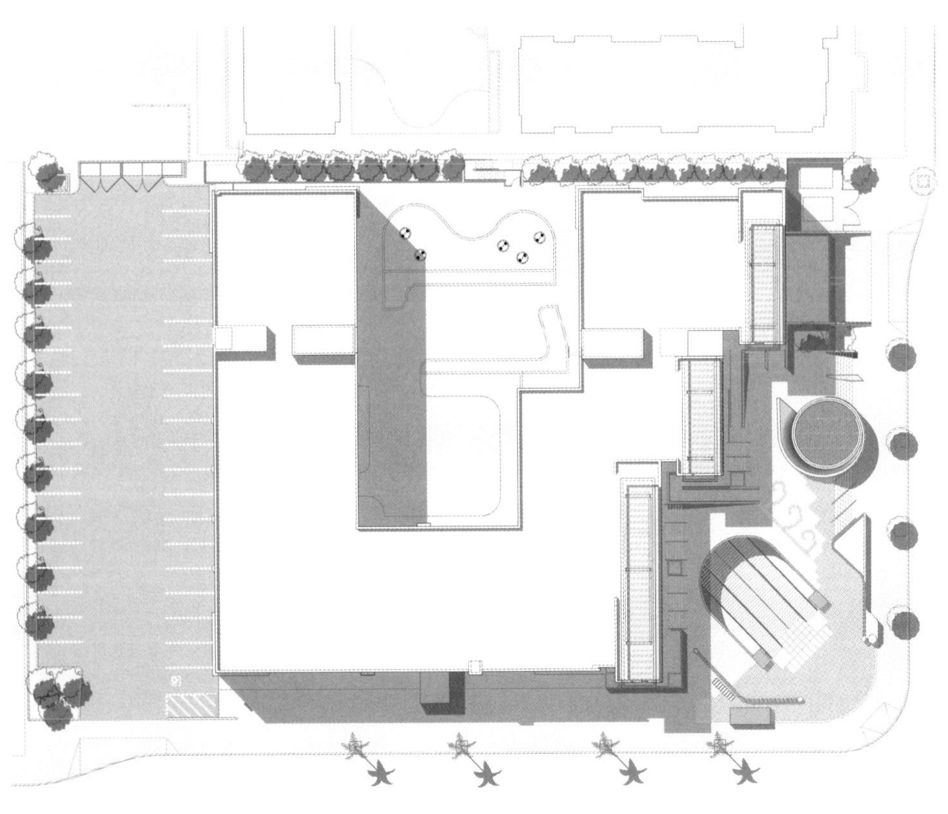

1672

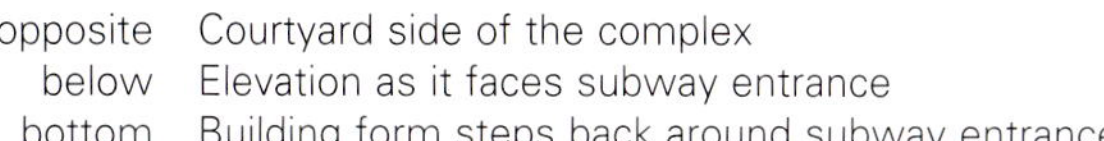
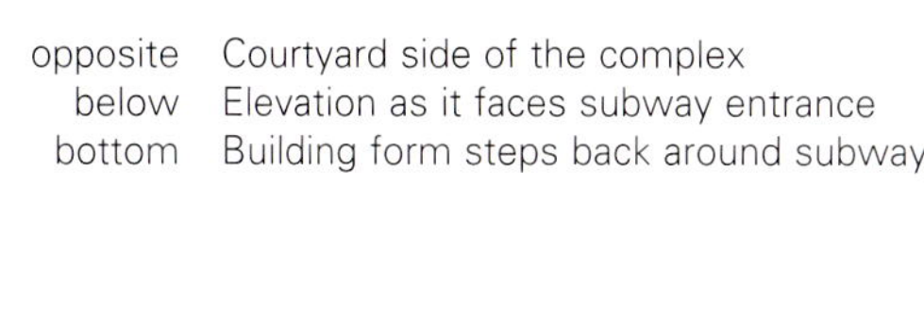

opposite Courtyard side of the complex
below Elevation as it faces subway entrance
bottom Building form steps back around subway entrance

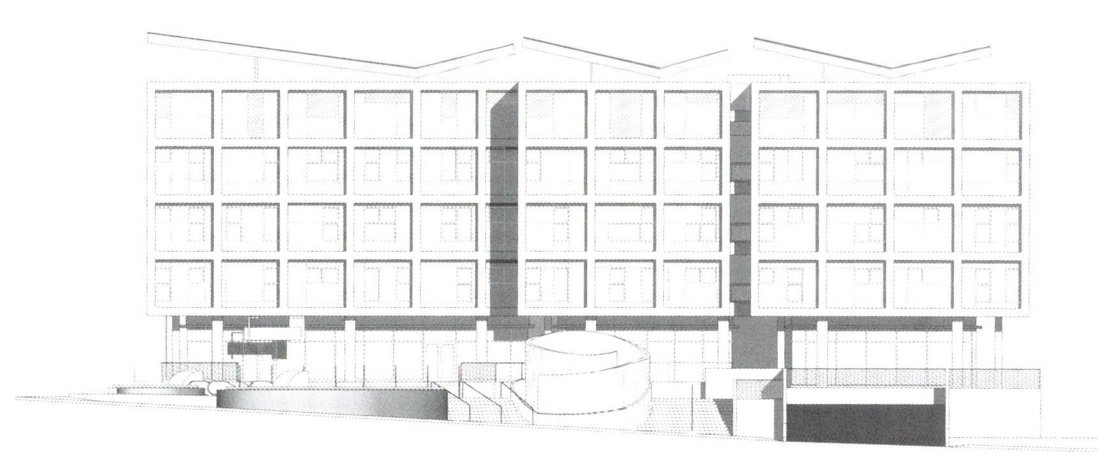

right Fenestration incorporates simple detailing
bottom Corner unit with butted glass windows
opposite Upper-level residential and lower-level retail plans
Photography John Edward Linden

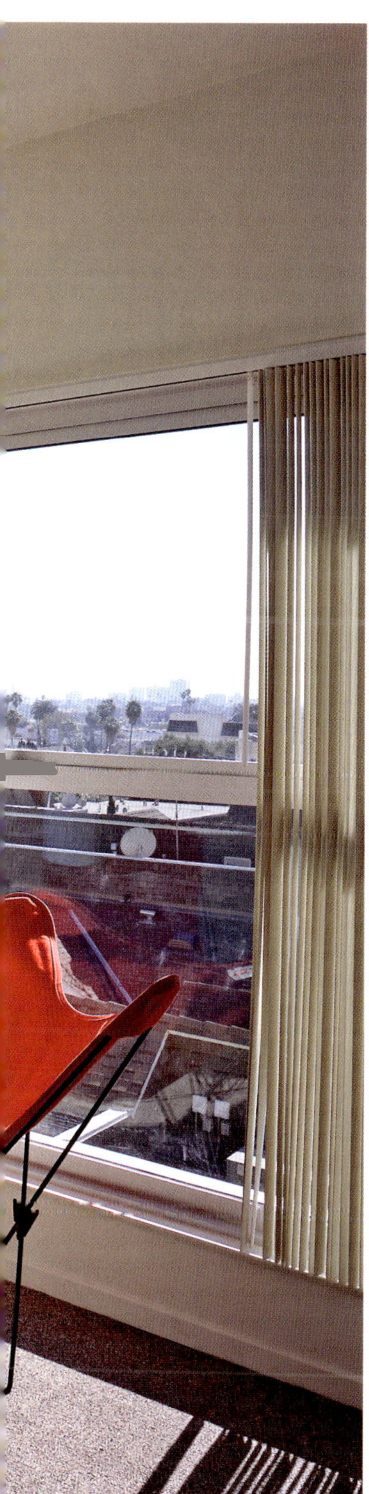

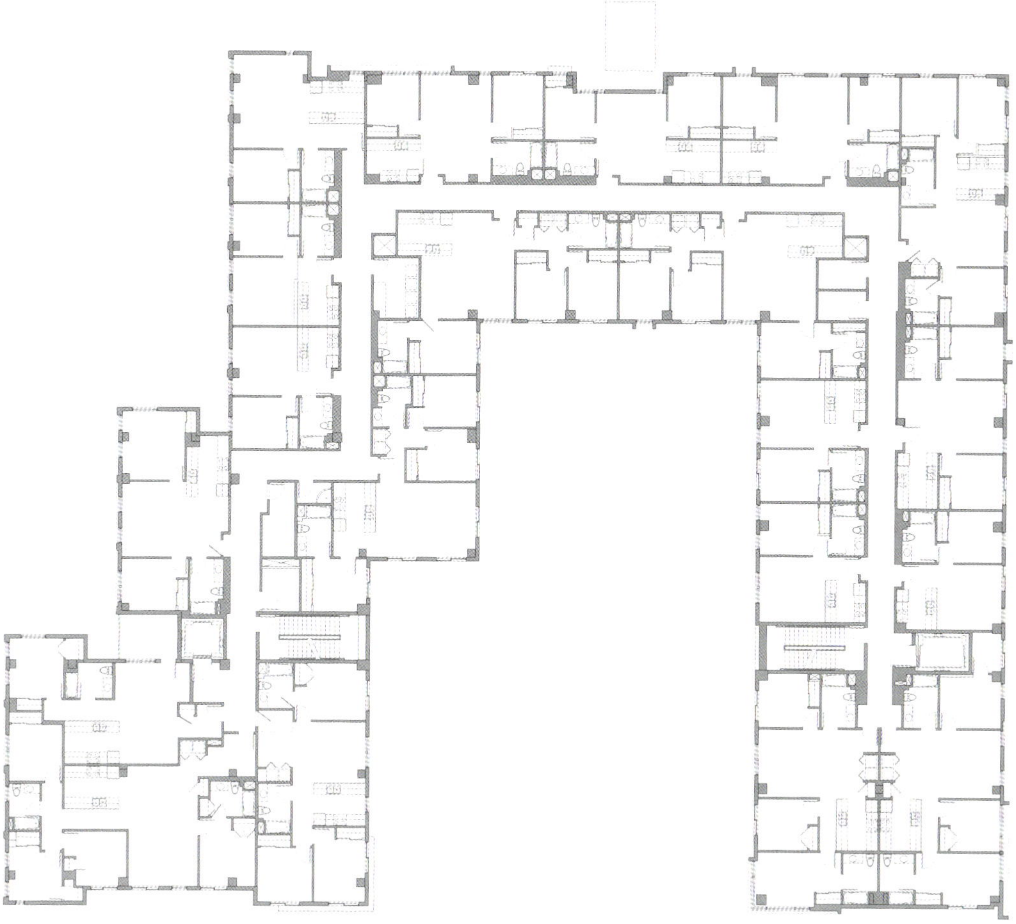

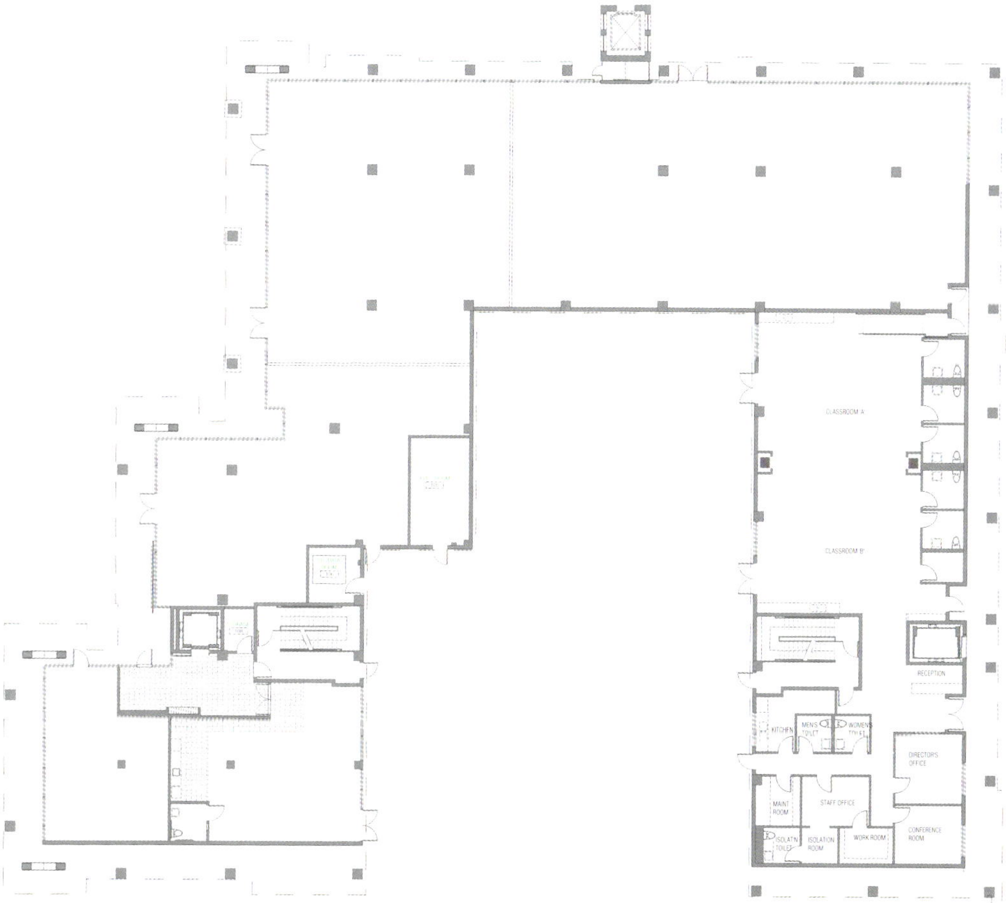
CLASSROOM 'A'
CLASSROOM 'B'
RECEPTION
KITCHEN
MEN'S TOILET
WOMEN'S TOILET
DIRECTOR'S OFFICE
MAINT ROOM
STAFF OFFICE
ISOLATN TOILET
ISOLATION ROOM
WORK ROOM
CONFERENCE ROOM

Contemporaine

Chicago, Illinois, USA

Perkins + Will

bottom Residences are above four stories of retail and parking
opposite Open volumes at roof lend a heroic stature

This 28-unit condominium building is located in the River North area of urban Chicago. The building consists of an 11-story residential tower and a four-story retail and parking base. The sculptural quality of the tower and the articulation of its functional parts work to mediate the building to the varying scales of the surrounding context.

The mass of the tower is broken down by a series of slots scored down the façade with small cantilevered balconies. The east façade undulates to further break the mass as well as to provide more opportunities for views of the city skyline. Concrete shear walls and the plane of the roof frame the design and provide a distinctive profile.

To bring the base to a pedestrian scale, the structure of the parking garage is exposed with floor-to-ceiling glass between the floor slabs, similar to the tower above. On the north side of the building the dynamic expression of the sloped ramps leading to the upper parking levels adds relief and movement to the otherwise rectilinear structure. At the entry corner the erosion of the mass, the projection of the cantilevered balconies above, and a 45-foot column all reinforce the urban energy of Contemporaine's surroundings.

A narrow slot separates the base and tower, allowing necessary transfers of the building systems as the floor programs change from residential to parking. This detail also provides an aesthetic dialogue between the two elements and allows for a reading of the building as a series of combined parts of varying scales. The top of the tower is sculpted to offer large terraces for the penthouse units and a gesture to the surrounding skyscrapers.

Typical floors at Contemporaine provide up to four condominiums with two and three-bedroom plans that can be combined to allow for larger units. Each unit has at least one private outdoor balcony. Unit sizes range from approximately 950 square feet to 2700 square feet. The open floor plans with large expanses of floor-to-ceiling glass allow natural light and dynamic views of the downtown skyline.

Binny's

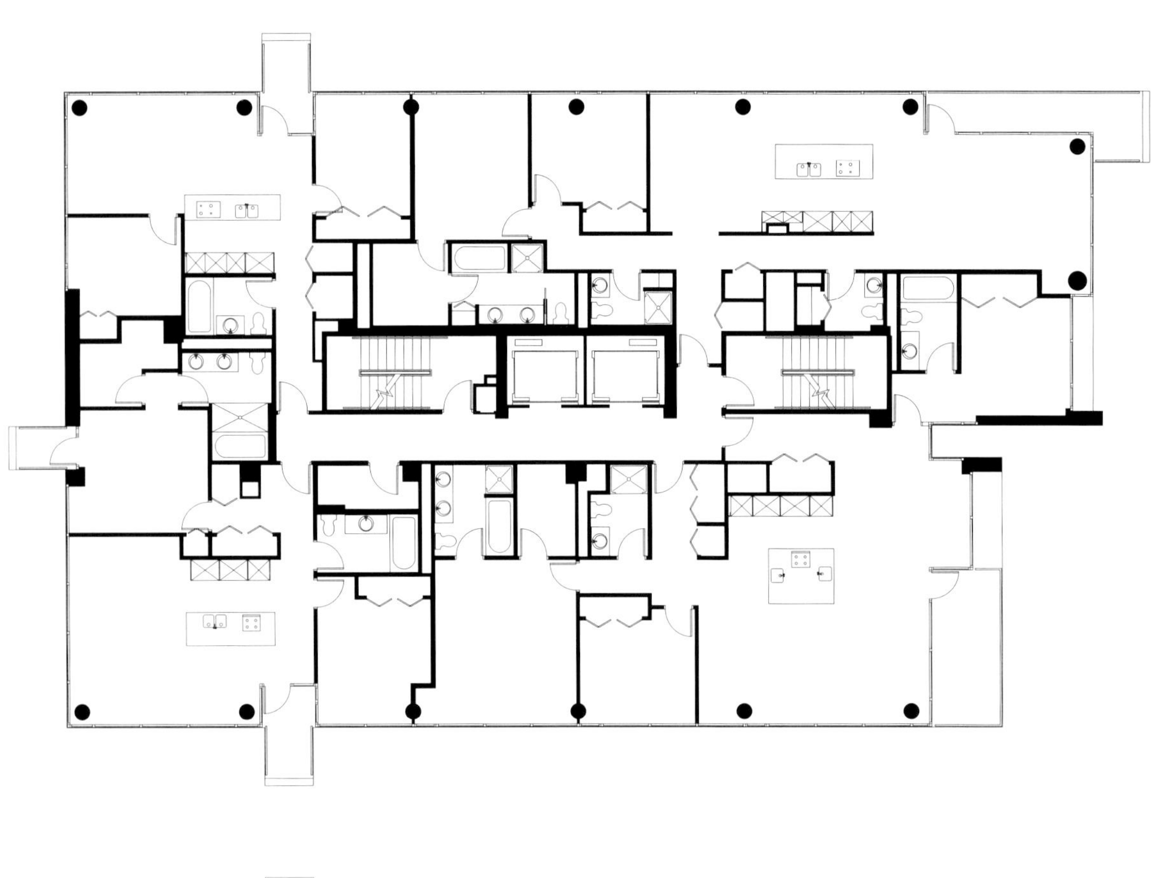

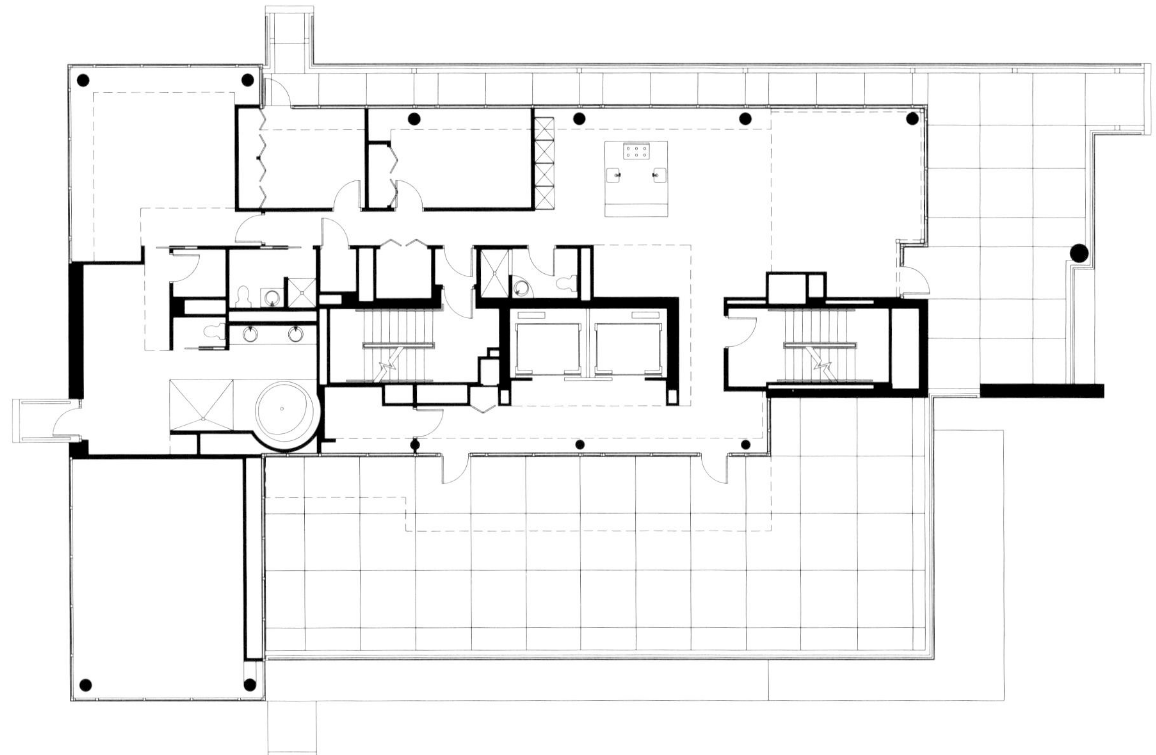

top Mid-level plan
above Penthouse plan
opposite left Concrete shear wall framed by glass
opposite right Private balconies punctuate each floor
opposite bottom Penthouse unit with generous roof terrace

Natarus

516

left	Residences jut out over garage and retail
bottom left	Concrete and glass on the Chicago skyline
bottom right	Sculptural array of concrete and glass
opposite	Spacious penthouse

opposite top	Each unit has at least one private balcony
opposite bottom	Floor-to-ceiling windows fill units with light and views
top	Penthouse has Chicago at its feet
Photography	© James @ Steinkamp Photography

Orange Grove
Lofts

West Hollywood, California, USA

Pugh + Scarpa Architecture

bottom Orange Grove in its West Hollywood context
opposite Façades are a play of geometric parts

Located in a neighborhood characterized by traditional bungalow-style, single-family residences, Orange Grove is sensitively designed and compatible with the neighborhood, but differs in material pallet and scale from its neighbors. Referencing architectural conventions of modernism rather than the pitched roof forms of traditional domesticity, the project presents a characteristic that is consistent with the eclectic and often unconventional demographic of West Hollywood. Distinct from neighboring structures, the building creates a strong relationship to the street by virtue of its large amount of highly usable balcony area in the front façade.

While there are dramatic and larger scale elements that define the building, it is also broken down into comprehensible human scale parts, and into two different buildings. Like the nearby Schindler House, the conventional architectural elements of windows and porches become part of an abstract sculptural ensemble. At the Schindler House, windows are found in the gaps between structural concrete wall panels. At Orange Grove, windows are inserted in gaps between different sections of the building.

Orange Grove's design is generated by a subtle balance of tensions. Building volumes and the placement of windows, doors, and balconies are not static but rather constitute an active three-dimensional composition in motion. Each piece of the building is a strong and clearly defined shape, such as the corrugated metal surround that encloses the second-story balcony in the east and north façades.

Another example of this clear delineation is the use of two square profile balcony surrounds in the front façade that set up a dialogue between them—one is small, the other large; one is open at the front, the other is veiled with stainless steel slats. At the same time each balcony is balanced and related to other elements in the building; the smaller one to the driveway gate below and the other to the roll-up door and first floor balcony. Each building element is intended to read as an abstract form in itself—such as a window becoming a slit or windows becoming a framed box, while also becoming part of a larger whole.

NO
PARKING
8AM TO 10AM
FRIDAYS
NO
PARKING

left Building pulls apart to create a courtyard
bottom Exterior forms inspired by Richard Neutra
opposite Third-, second-, and first-floor plans
opposite left Views framed by horizontal windows
opposite right Living level with stair to mezzanine

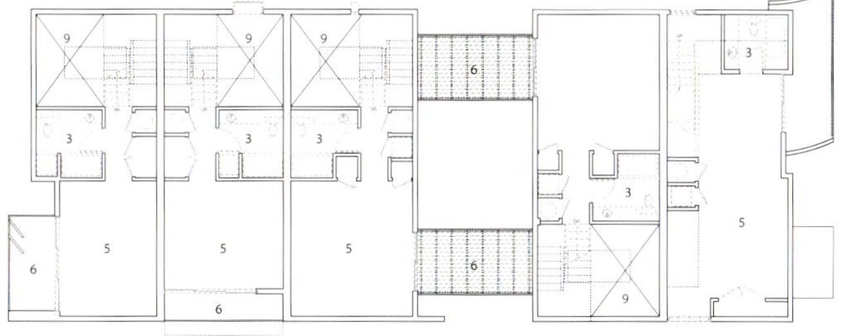

1 Living room
2 Kitchen
3 Bathroom
4 Mezzanine
5 Bedroom
6 Balcony
7 Courtyard
8 Driveway
9 Open
10 Adjacent building

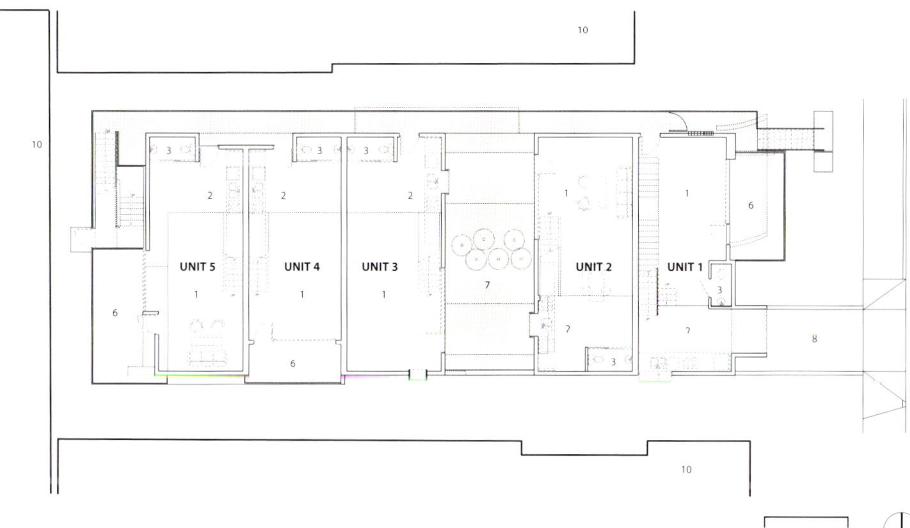

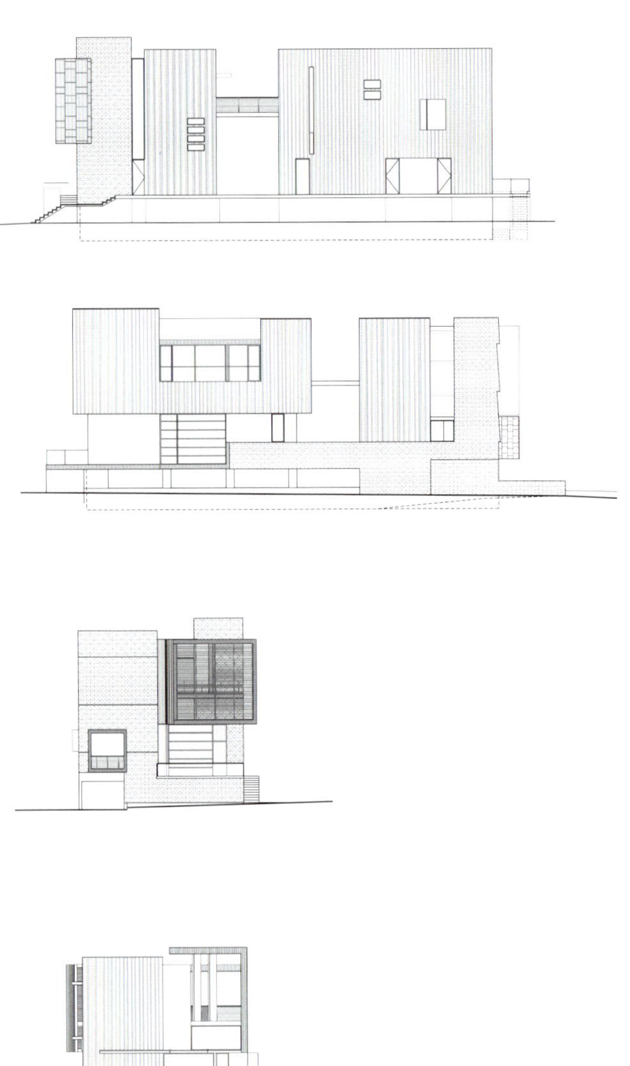

opposite top	Geometric elements interrelate in elevation
far left	Stair scales the interior wall
left	View from bedroom level to kitchen in Unit 1
top	Interiors are containers of abundant space
Photography	Marvin Rand

Solaire

New York, New York, USA

Pelli Clarke Pelli Architects

bottom Solaire in its Battery Park City neighborhood
opposite top Overlooking a park and the river beyond
opposite bottom Solaire as viewed from the river

Located in Battery Park City overlooking the Hudson River at the southern tip of Manhattan, this 293-unit, 27-story apartment building is the first to be designed under an ambitious set of guidelines developed by the Battery Park City Authority and modeled on the U.S. Green Building Council's LEED rating system (which stands for Leadership in Energy and Environmental Design). As the first "green" high-rise residential building in the US, it is a model for other such developments. Steven Winter Associates, Inc. served as the Solaire's sustainability consultant.

The design incorporates several technologies and systems that promote sustainability: photovoltaics, blackwater treatment, gas absorption chillers, and occupancy sensor systems for both lighting and climate control. The design reduces overall energy use by 35 percent beyond New York State energy code requirements. The building-integrated photovoltaics create five percent of the base-building electricity. The blackwater treatment plant provides recycled water for use in toilets and in the cooling tower, which reduces the use of potable water by 38 percent. Rooftop gardens reduce stormwater runoff by half. A significant number of the building materials with a high recycled content and low or no VOCs were purchased within a 500-mile radius of New York City.

The building is Gold LEED Certified and was selected as one of the American Institute of Architects' Top Ten Green Projects for 2004 by AIA's Committee on the Environment. The Solaire is one of the first buildings to receive funding under the New York State Green Building Tax Credit. It was also chosen by the U.S. Department of Energy to represent America in Oslo, Norway, for the 2002 Green Building Challenge, an international conference on sustainable technology.

top — The Solaire is the first in a multi-building development
right — Natural light is maximized for interiors
opposite top — Vegetated roof terraces reduce water runoff
opposite bottom — Typical floor plan
Photography — Jeff Goldberg / Esto Photographics

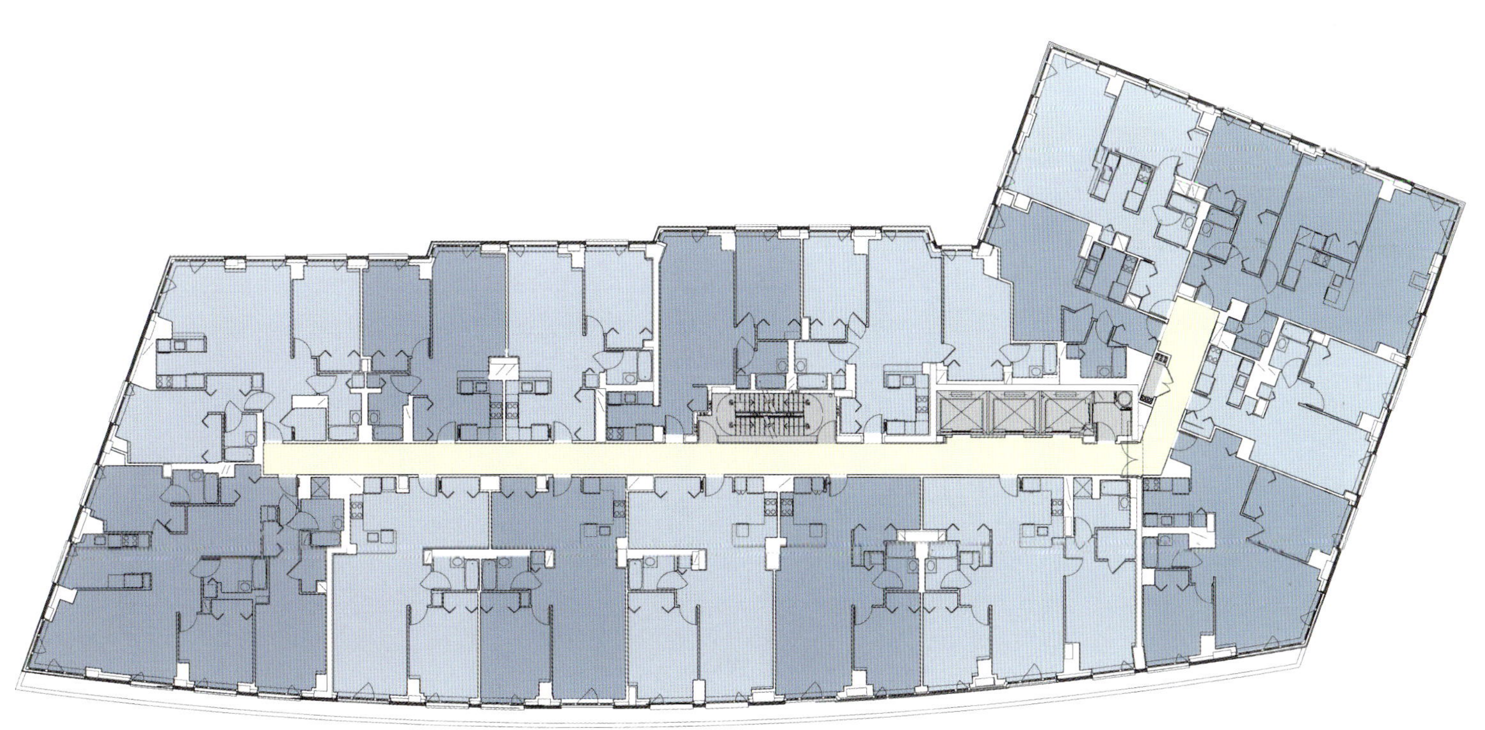

1212 Euclid

Santa Monica, California, USA

David Forbes Hibbert, Architect

bottom Courtyard planting helps alleviate water runoff
opposite top The complex maintains the neighborhood's low scale
opposite bottom Open walkways lead to units

This apartment building is designed for young professionals and is located in a medium density residential neighborhood adjacent to downtown Santa Monica. There are three buildings, each two stories tall, connected by open-air walkways and arranged to form a courtyard. There are a total of 13 apartments, each accessed by an individual exterior front door located at the courtyard side of the unit. At the opposite side of the unit are individual rear private decks or terraces. The combination of landscaping at both the courtyard side and rear of the units, the full-height glass windows and sliding doors, the nine-foot ceiling heights, and the front and rear door arrangement are meant to give the units an open quality that is part of a modern Southern Californian residential tradition of indoor-outdoor living.

The horizontal lines of the siding, eaves and canopies, and the detailing of interior cabinetry and doors pay respect to the vocabulary of the local 1950's and 1960's era residential buildings and California's famous Case Study Houses. Metal screens, open steel stairs, steel roof access ladders, and metal component hardware are all exposed in the contemporary tradition of Los Angeles with its influential aesthetic of raw industrial and economical functionality.

The parking is subterranean with the buildings and landscaping resting on a structural deck above. Water runoff is partially mitigated by the abundance and density of the planting. The parking ramp and building utility services are off the alley at the rear of the buildings. The emphasis on the quality of building frontage and green space, comprised of drought-tolerant self-sustaining planting, along with the de-emphasis on the automobile, are part the City of Santa Monica's more recent efforts to accent its environmental goals. The building adopts the goals of a new Santa Monica and Southern California architectural credo of sustainability and the influence of a regional residential architectural tradition, to create space for the lifestyles of its present community.

202

left Green spaces are part of courtyard design
top Upper and lower floor plans

right Unit plans connect with outdoor spaces
bottom Steel mesh railings suggest California design tradition
opposite Kitchen interiors are clean and elegant
Photography Benny Chan / Fotoworks

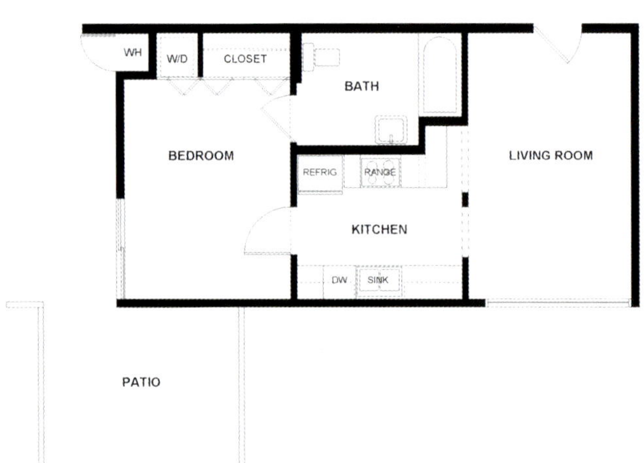

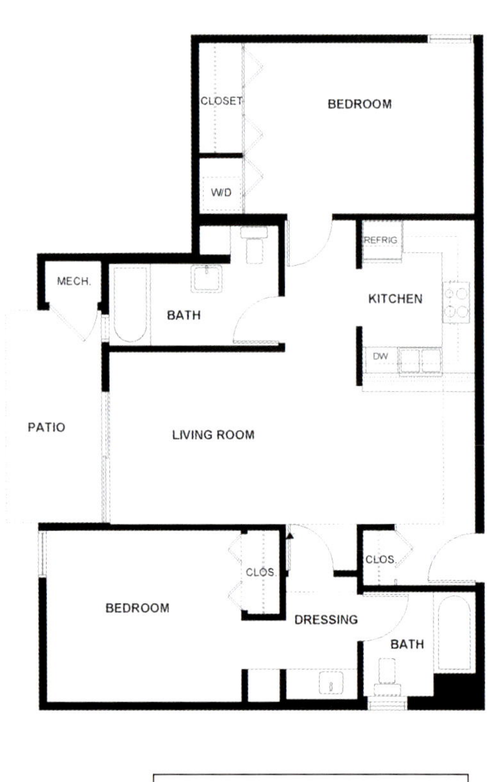

Radio City

Toronto, Ontario, Canada

architectsAlliance

bottom Site plan shows new building in darker color
opposite Towers as they surmount lower-level development

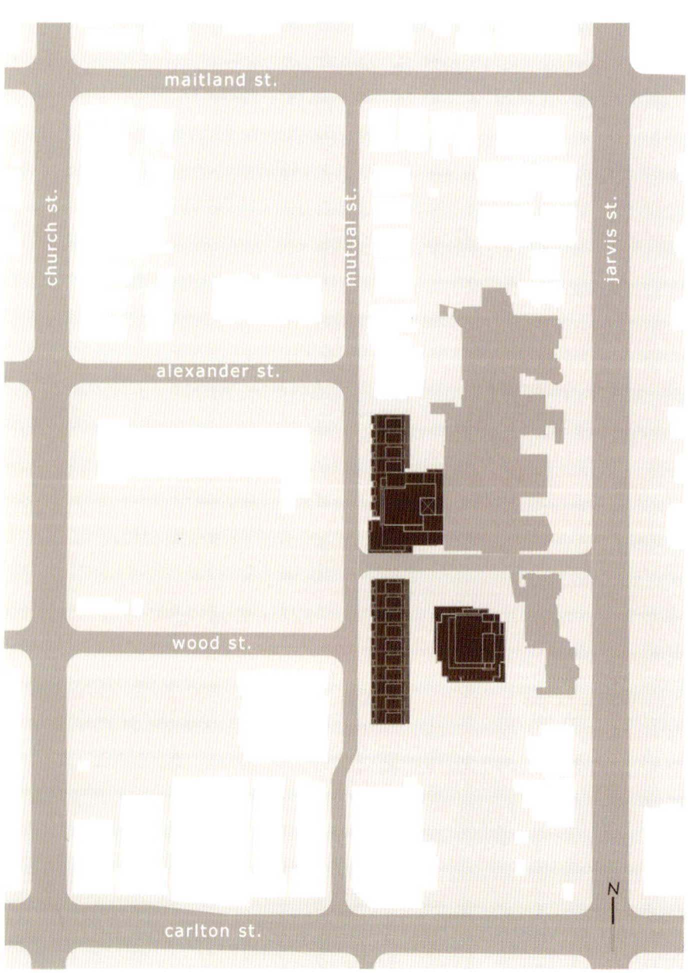

The Radio City condominium project is one of the two components of a complex residential/institutional development that has been integrated into an historic neighborhood on Jarvis Street in Toronto's downtown core.

The architects have created a 32,515-square-meter multi-unit residential complex, consisting of two small floor plate point towers, and a series of three-story townhouses that form a lower built form edge along Mutual Street. Two landscaped courtyards create a bridge between Radio City and the new National Ballet School (NBS), the other element in this innovative revitalization scheme, and help form a mid-block connection between Mutual and Jarvis streets.

The site comprises the former Havergal College and Longfield House, the former national headquarters of the Canadian Broadcasting Corporation. The client purchased the site from the CBC when that institution moved to its new home on Front Street in 1997. The client, in turn, sold half of the site area to the National Ballet School for $1. Consequently, the massing of the available residential density was allocated to half of the original site. The design of the Radio City project was deeply influenced by this reduction in the original land parcel, by the unique qualities of the existing heritage buildings on site, and by the character of the surrounding 19th-century residential streets.

The primary elements of the project are the two towers, 25 and 30 stories in height, respectively, extensively clad in glass and steel. Their slenderness (floor plates are 650 square meters) minimizes their apparent bulk, as does the positioning of the buildings back from the street edge.

The architects were careful not to disturb the existing residential scale on surrounding side streets. Three-story townhouses along Mutual Street echo the roofline and form of the adjacent Victorian row houses. The arrangement of buildings creates an interior court as a vehicular and pedestrian address for the project, and a pair of linked courtyards connecting to the NBS complex.

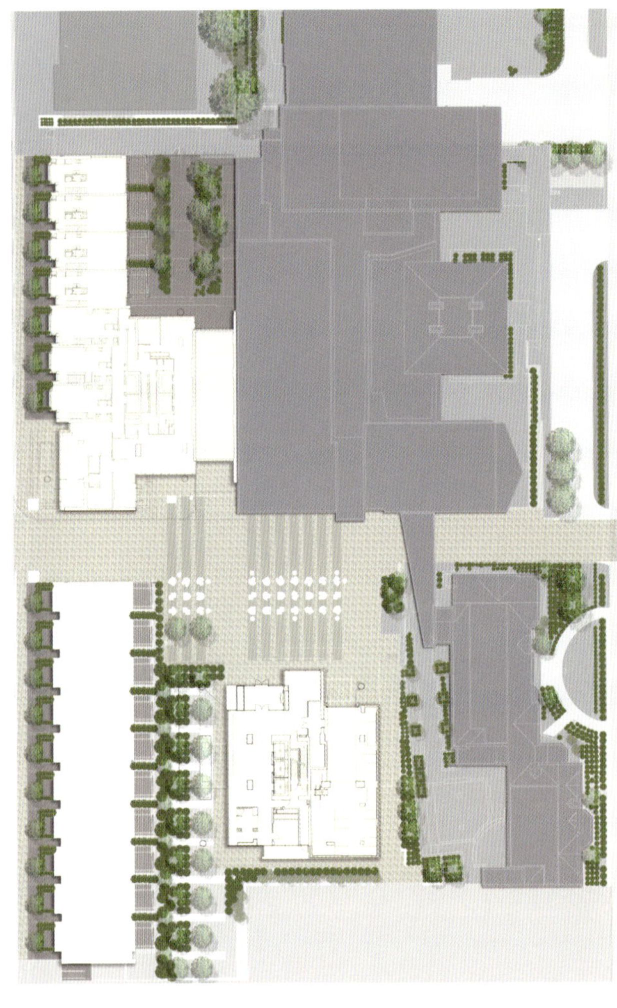

left Plans show townhouses with towers to right
bottom left Towers with nearby Victorian context
bottom Lower-rise units in front of towers

bottom	Street scale is maintained by lower-rise units
opposite left	Detail of townhouse entries
opposite right	Balconies break down plane of tower
opposite bottom	Overview of towers with low-rise units at left
Photography	Tom Arban

Italian Gardens

San Jose, California, USA

Seidel Holzman

bottom Site plan incorporates existing buildings
opposite Units are organized around small courtyards

This affordable housing community occupies an irregularly shaped six-acre parcel near downtown San Jose. Formerly occupied by an Italian restaurant, the site had several notable features including Italian grotto gardens, heritage trees, and an historical home. All were incorporated as part of the new design.

Key to the project's successful planning is an urban density that helps to foster a sense of community identity. A high proportion of two-and three-bedroom apartments accommodate families earning below the median income for the area. Each unit has its own individual exterior entry and patio. Many of the apartments are oriented toward a large landscaped common area at the center of the project. The central pedestrian path connects a number of amenities for the residents, including several tot lots, an olive grove, a computer learning center, a swimming pool, and the restored gardens. A second community building accommodates a senior meal program for on and off-site residents.

The pedestrian path also connects into the city street system. The northern edge of the courtyard is anchored by a pair of taller tower-like building elements. Passing through these and out toward Almaden Boulevard, one has easy pedestrian access to the Tamian Station on San Jose's light rail line. This provides the Italian Gardens' residents with convenient and economical transportation to employment, shopping, and recreation.

Special attention was given to utilizing low-cost materials creatively to give the project variety and distinction. Various wood siding types painted in contrasting colors accent the project massing and help establish a pleasant neighborhood scale.

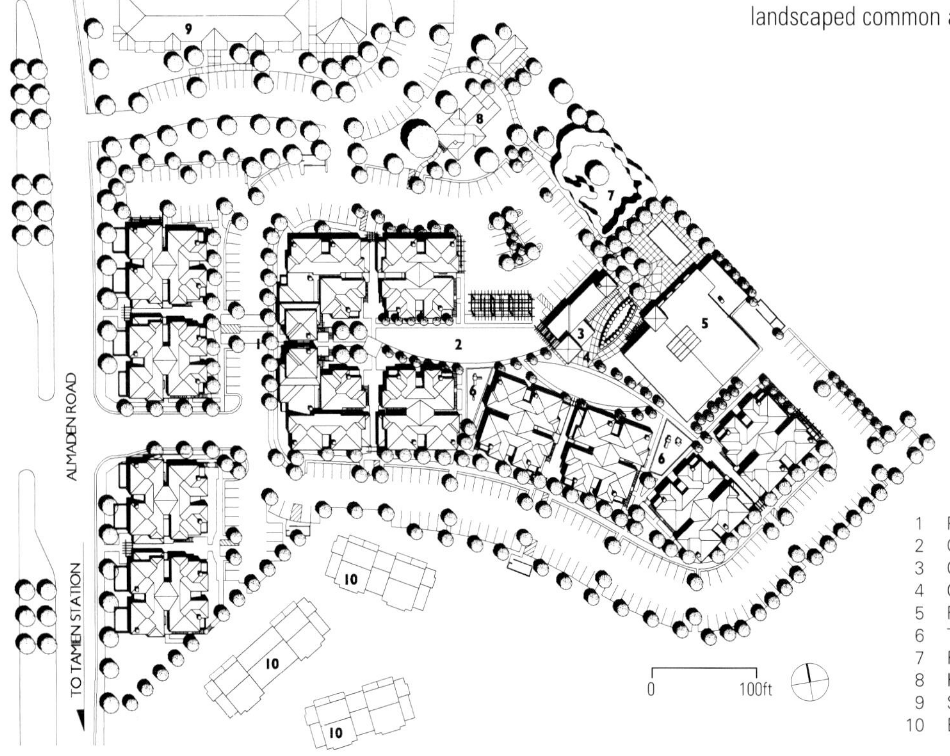

1 Pedestrian gateway
2 Community common green
3 Computer learning center and leasing facility
4 Community plaza
5 Future community facility
6 Tot lot
7 Restored historic garden
8 Historic Locurio House community facility
9 Senior apartment
10 Existing condominiums

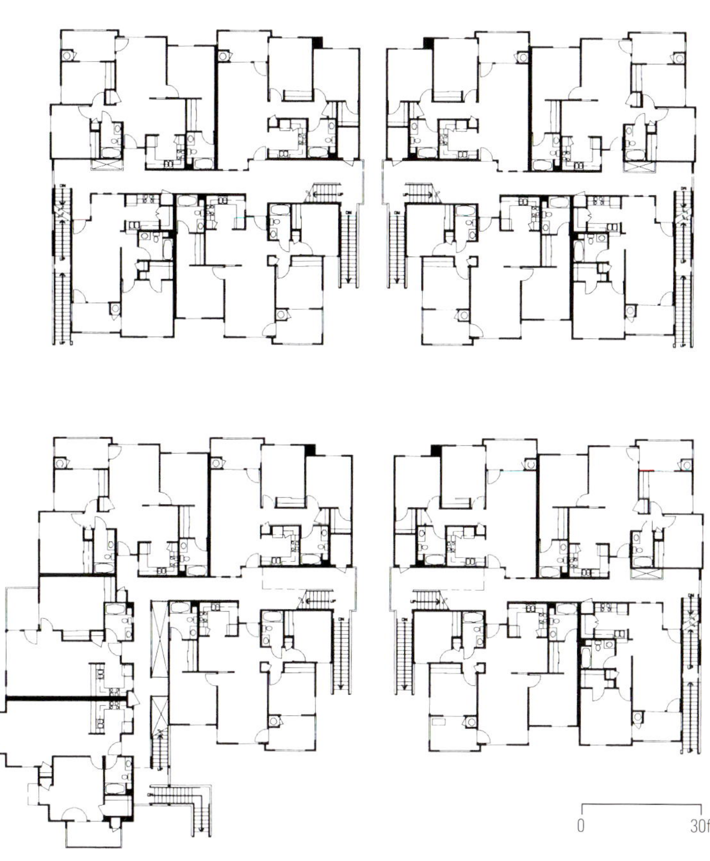

above Unit plans
left Landscaped areas extend through site

top Section through apartment building
bottom A sense of community is fostered despite the high density
opposite top Each unit has private outdoor space
opposite bottom Units look onto common green space
Photography Tom Rider

Folsom Dore

San Francisco, California, USA

David Baker + Partners

bottom Design incorporates an existing brick warehouse façade
opposite top Unit balconies overlook the busy street
opposite bottom Units step back as the building turns the corner

The Folsom Dore project consists of the creation of 98 new apartment units in an existing building that are affordable to residents at or below 60 percent of the area median income. The site is in the city's South of Market neighborhood, which includes a diverse mix of residential, commercial, and light industrial uses. The units are a mix of one-bedroom and two-bedroom studios ranging in size from approximately 500 to 800 square feet. Many of the units are targeted to residents with a wide range of special needs such as physical or developmental disabilities, HIV/AIDS illness, chronic unemployment, and people living on low incomes.

The development is four levels of frame construction over a Type I concrete structure. It includes 30 parking spaces in a single-level, partially submerged garage and approximately 3200 square feet of flexible community space that houses on-site programs and services along Folsom Street. The existing building was partially retained to help integrate the overall project with the surrounding neighborhood. There is approximately 3500 square feet of open space, which includes a front entry courtyard as well as a ground level courtyard in the rear of the development.

The entry garden court and "green" stair provide a transitional decompression space to mitigate between the hard urban exterior environment and the new dwellings. Giant bamboo grows inside the stairway, reaching the top floors.

Part of a demolished brick warehouse structure has been recycled into a storefront along the main Folsom Street frontage to provide a more prominent presence for the community meeting room and to collage part of the history of this space into the new design.

The design provides a 14-car garage serving the neighborhood to support the local businesses located along Dore Street. Residential parking for residents is reduced to 12 spaces, a car-share pod with four shared cars, and 28 bicycle spaces.

75

opposite Mid-block entry to stairway leading to units
left Open stair for unit access
below Community space faces onto street
middle Upper-level unit plans
bottom Ground-level plan
Photography Michelle Peckham

1 Rear yard
2 Playground area
3 Storage
4 Laundry
5 Janitor
6 Units
7 Trash/recycling
8 Storage
9 Office
10 Mechanical

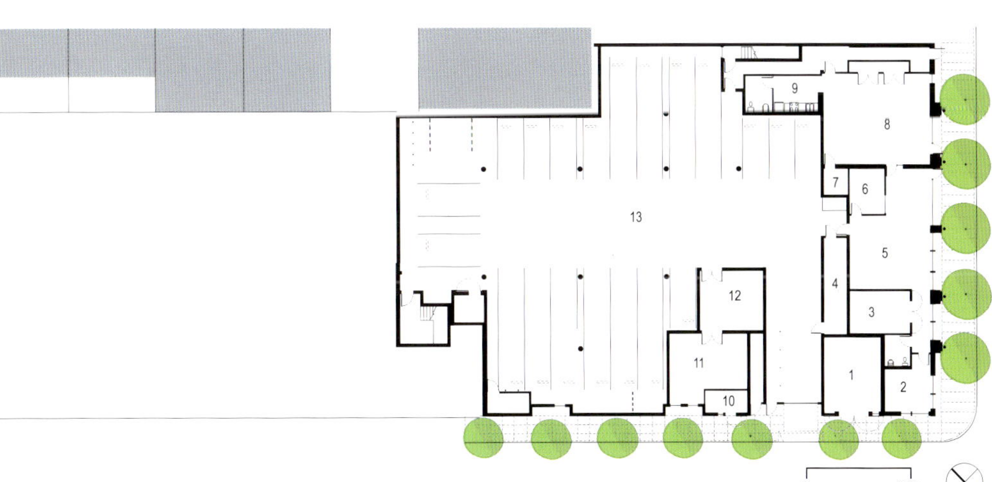

1 Transformer
2 Office
3 Classroom
4 Electrical
5 Multipurpose office
6 Office
7 Storage
8 Multipurpose community
9 Kitchen
10 Gas
11 Mechanical
12 Trash/recycling
13 Parking garage

North Court

Boulder, Colorado, USA

Wolff Lyon Architects

bottom	Exteriors are inspired by local farmhouses
opposite top	Each unit has an identifiable entrance
opposite left	Interiors are light-filled and simple
opposite right	Low walls and paths connect buildings
opposite bottom	Site plan has neighborhood quality
Photography	John Wolff

North Court is an exemplary mixed-income residential and work studio community. Sixty-eight one-, two-, and three-bedroom residences along with nine 730-square-foot workspaces are distributed in 12 separate buildings along traditional neighborhood streets. There are three different building models containing five, six, and seven units arranged with different configurations and heights. Forty percent of the residential units are deed-restricted to low income households. The overall net density on the 2.7-acre-site is 28.5 dwelling units per acre.

The collection of buildings is designed so that each elevation has a strong presence and orientation to a street as well as a courtyard. Individual porches and front entries on every side welcome residents and visitors. Common corridors and lobbies are eliminated, helping to reduce construction cost and on-going maintenance. Buildings are arranged to create well-defined public realms. A sense of community is promoted through the courtyards with each creating a memorable outdoor room. Opportunities for casual encounters and neighborly interaction are encouraged through large covered porches on both the first and second stories. Special attention was given to the low natural sandstone walls that deal with the grade changes on the site and provide a framework for landscaping treatments.

The architecture is inspired by the simple architectural precedents often found on agricultural buildings, translated into building forms appropriate for Colorado and the setting. Three significantly different building designs are mixed to create diversity of unit type and architectural interest. The building architecture helps express the individual identity of each residence through form and color.

North Court illustrates that high-quality mixed-income development is possible even with the constraints of limited land area, a mix of uses, and a large number of affordable units.

Parent Avenue
Lofts

Royal Oak, Michigan, USA

McIntosh Poris Associates

bottom Former lumber warehouse is now housing
opposite Lofts created with exposed wood framing

This project is an adaptive reuse of a former lumber warehouse, which was converted into eight for-sale residential units. The shell of the 9412-square-foot structure was left largely intact and divided into two-level loft units that range from 1264 to 2225 square feet (excluding garages).

The building's industrial character was preserved while introducing contemporary design elements. The units are refined and architecturally stylized with industrial influences, such as exposed duct work, 21-foot-high ceilings, metal-roof trusses, concrete floors on the ground level, and open, flexible spaces.

The introduction of new design elements maintains the integrity of an urban loft, while also providing homeowners privacy, space, and comfort. New design elements include kitchen, bathroom, bedroom, and living spaces; the creation of a mezzanine level; floor-to-ceiling window walls; pyramidal skylights; maple wood flooring on the mezzanine level; custom-designed railings and staircases made of maple-wood and steel; and exposed wood framing over the kitchen.

The original masonry block exterior façade had no windows and only a few overhead doors. The entire front wall was removed and reconstructed in steel and clad in cement masonry units. The new sand-colored, cement-block façade reflects the structure's original industrial use. To balance the façade, the architects added warm design elements, such as orange-colored box-bay windows on the second level, which are constructed of Parklex 1000 wood veneer sheets.

Each unit has two levels, both open and flexible, with a private entry way, attached garage, powder room, and an elongated hallway that leads deeper into the interior to the custom-designed kitchen and open living space organized in the rear. Twenty-one-foot-high window walls at the south end of the units bring natural light directly into living and dining spaces. A custom-designed metal-and-wood staircase connects to the second level, which features flexible mezzanine loft space overlooking the first floor.

A master bedroom and adjacent bathroom are located toward the front of the second floor (over the garage). This configuration provides more privacy in the bedrooms, which are on the north-end of the building—away from the single-family residences to the building's south.

right	Front façade includes colorful bay windows
below left	Ground-level plan
below right	Second-floor plan
bottom	Living area is found to rear of unit
opposite top	View from living area to front entry
opposite bottom	Tall windows fill spaces with light

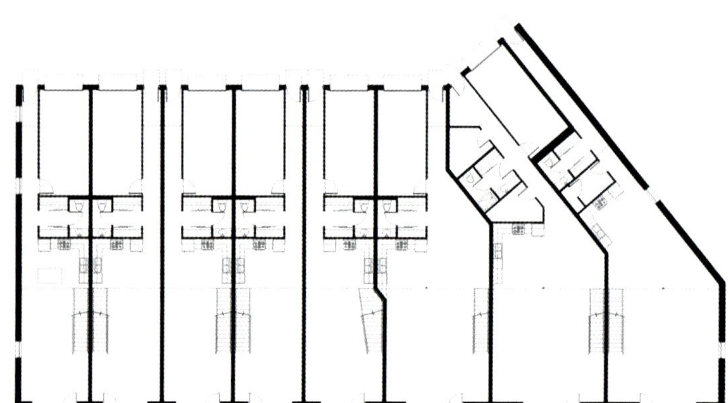

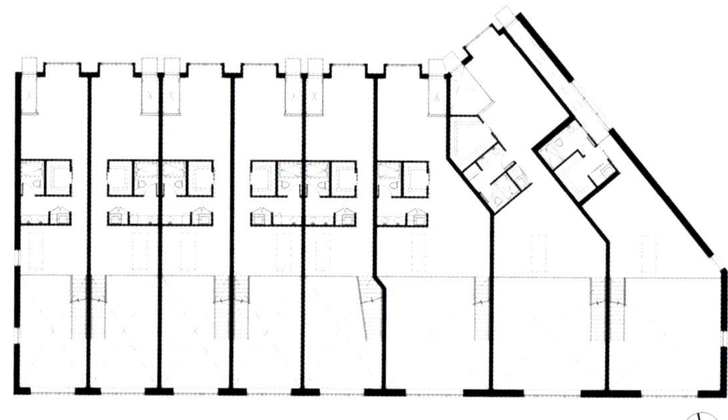

top left	East-end units feature angled walls
top right	Bathrooms feature utilitarian fixtures
bottom left	Ground-level features concrete floors
bottom right	Kitchens are tucked under mezzanine
opposite top	Bedroom has ample storage
opposite bottom	Mezzanine's freestanding bathroom and closet

Waterloo Heights

Los Angeles, California, USA

Koning Eizenberg Architecture

bottom Courtyard is at the heart of the complex
opposite Exterior is a mix of stucco and wood siding

Designed for a non-profit developer, Waterloo Heights Apartments navigates a multitude of funding-source requirements including HUD, the Los Angeles Community Design Commission and the Los Angeles Housing Department, while negotiating a public review process that achieved a 100 percent density bonus. Within affordable housing parameters, the design creates a successful relationship to context in image, building massing, articulation, and detail and is expected to serve as a model for similar infill projects. Most importantly, the special-needs tenant group, which includes the disabled, HIV individuals, seniors and veterans, enjoy living there.

Designed through a series of community meetings with neighbors concerned about density and traffic, this 18-unit project (11 one-bedroom units and seven studios) focuses on a central courtyard/ gathering spot for residents surrounded by a community room, manager's office, and laundry facility. The court overlooks the entry for security. The location of the property at the crest of a small hill allows for downtown views.

The scheme of four small buildings around a court is patterned after Craftsman Style bungalows and Spanish courtyard housing in the area. A hybrid of stucco and board-and-batten siding materials bridge stylistic gaps found in the neighborhood. Simultaneously, the division of the buildings mirrors the scale and mix of adjacent single-family residences and apartments. The elevation along Waterloo Street articulates 10 units into a composition that appears as two to three homes, continuing the rhythm of properties northward. A palette of warm creamy stucco with dark-gray/green wood siding creates a calm neighborly building. Accents are provided by lime-green doors and flowering planting. Simple metal railings are augmented with accented wood boards to break the monotony and institutional feeling of "miles of guardrails." Trellis elements provide armatures for climbing wisteria vines. Exterior spaces are carefully lit with shielded light sources and tree uplights to maintain residential qualities.

A community room and laundry with a large siding door open to the court and management office are cut into the hillside behind a retaining wall. Floor levels step down in response to the sloping site, but all areas of the site and every unit is fully accessible.

1011

opposite top	Units are entered directly from outside
opposite bottom	Composition echoes nearby houses
left	Low walls, fences, and balconies provide semi-public space
bottom left	Ground-level plan
bottom right	Upper-level plan
Photography	Lucy Gonzalez

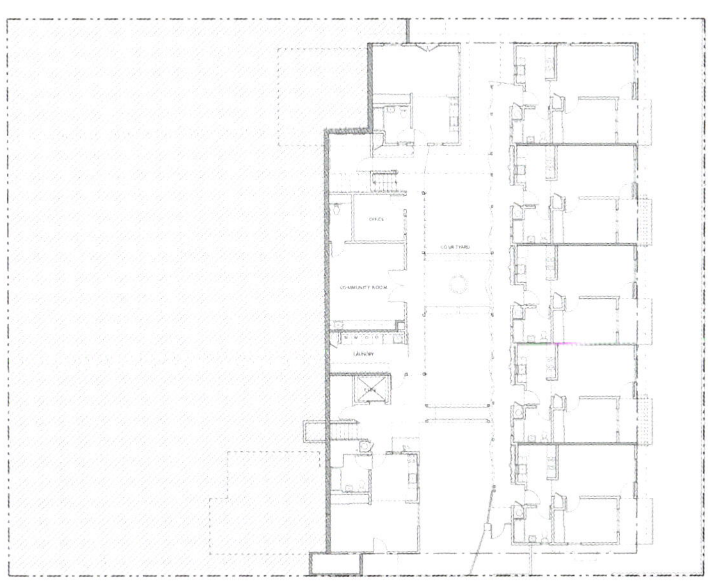

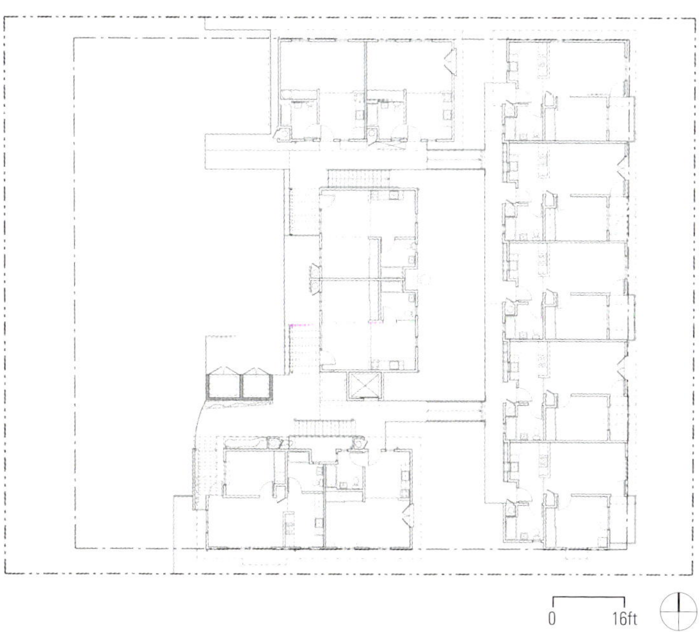

0 16ft

Brownstones
at Riverfront Park

Denver, Colorado, USA

Humphries Poli Architects

This project's relatively small size (a three-story building comprising 16 units) belies its big role in adding depth and interest to Denver's cityscape. Clad in buff-colored sandstone and ebony-colored brick, accented with painted aluminum and resplendent with wide areas of mullioned windows, the project is a unique mixture of urban living strategies including accessibility, individuality, security, and a strong connection to the surrounding community.

These shared-wall, single-family homes have individual entrances, unique floor plans, separate and secure garages, and differentiated exteriors. They are also hybrids that put a new gloss on the time-tested idea of brownstones, skillfully applying the grand proportions and excellent craftsmanship of their namesakes to indoor/outdoor living spaces uniquely suited to a dry, sunny climate. The exteriors respond to local historical and architectural precedents, acting as a perfect foil to the units' modern interiors and amenities.

Living spaces gradually open up from the inside to outside. The most private interior spaces give way to semi-private exterior areas such as balconies and patios, which, in turn, interface with increasingly more public spaces: the courtyard, the street, the park, and, finally, the city itself. The courtyard at the heart of the project offers both private gardens and a landscaped gathering space for residents.

There are three separate plans varying from 2400 to 5400 square feet. Windows and light are used as prominent design elements. Large glazed areas, coupled with ample volumes, bring in generous amounts of daylight to give units the feel of a detached home.

bottom Earth tones tie the buildings to the site
opposite Individual entrances to each unit from the street

2131

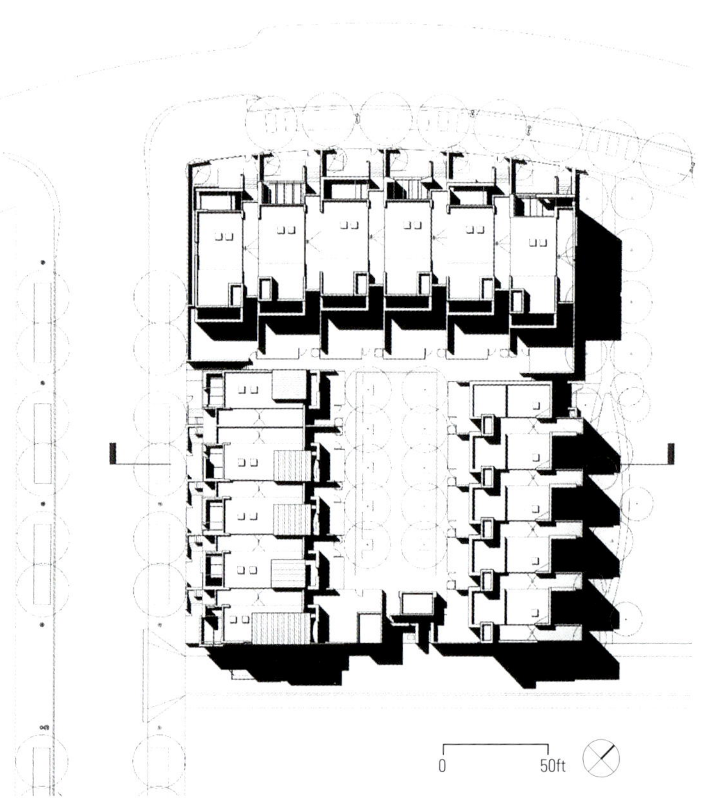

top left Site plan of complex
top Townhouses back on to a semi-public courtyard
opposite left A variety of materials play off of each other
opposite right Scale is broken down through low walls

top	Open floor plan on main level
right	Townhouses' simple yet abstract forms
opposite top	Three-level unit plans with top, entry, and bottom floor
opposite bottom	Interior colors echo exteriors
Photography	Ed LaCasse

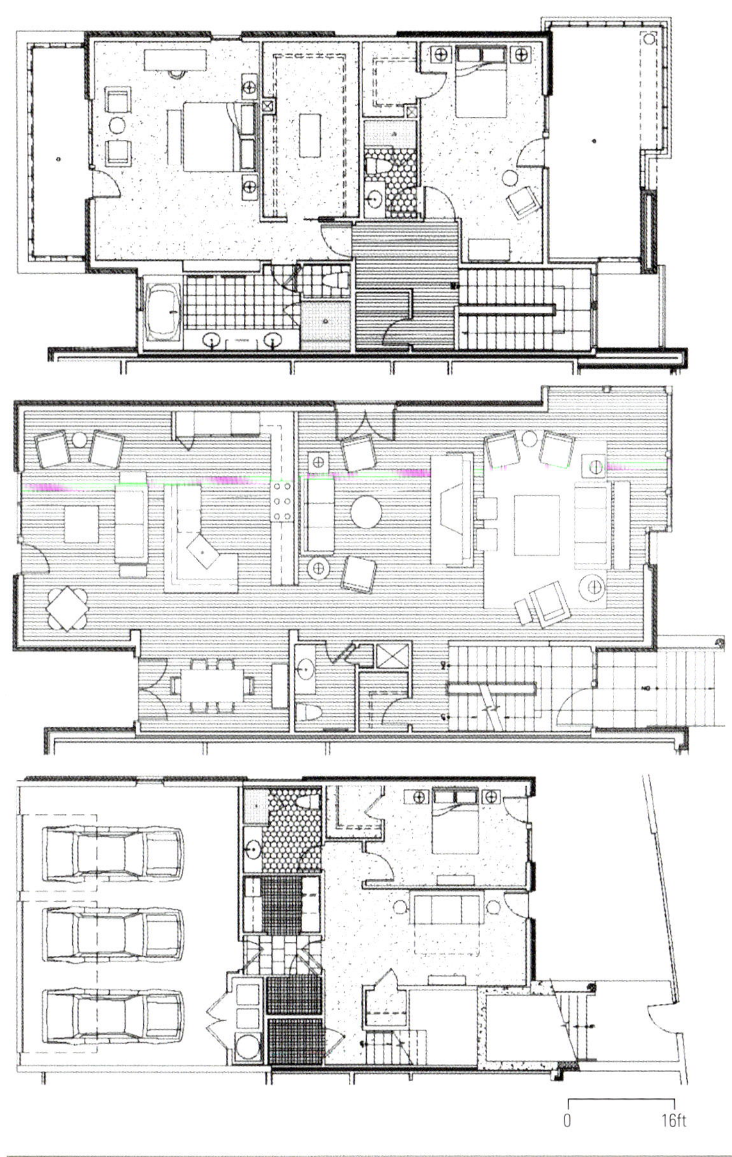
0
16ft

Bergamot
Artist Lofts

Santa Monica, California, USA

Pugh + Scarpa Architecture

bottom Metal siding underscores building's industrial character
opposite Living spaces are open and flexible

Bergamot Station is an internationally known art center comprised of a series of industrial buildings converted into 45 art galleries including the Santa Monica Museum of Art. The program includes a ground-level studio/gallery space with three artist live/work loft spaces above.

The fundamental challenge in this project was determining how to maintain continuity and coherence with the character of the existing industrial warehouse buildings at Bergamot Station without compromising formal and material experimentation and innovation. Corrugated metal, steel, and glass blend in with the surrounding context while cold-rolled steel and translucent Lexan panels create moments of distinction in the details of the building that set it apart and help establish its idiosyncratic identity.

The exterior never strays far from its industrial origins and therefore maintains a respectful coherence with its context. The façade facing the interior of the site unfolds itself gracefully along a canted corrugated metal plane that extends itself into the residual space produced by the adjacent buildings. The building's south-facing façade, which fronts the public street, provides a personality foil for its more geometrically complex and dynamic counterpart on the Arts Complex facing façade.

The ground floor's open plan allows maximum flexibility. A separate entrance leads to the three artist loft units above of 1250 square feet. Each of these maximizes its potential for spaciousness and light while also creating moments of intimacy and enclosure. Each unit has a fluidity of space and circulation that creates a sensation of open airiness even though they are flanked between buildings on either side and only feature minimal windows to the outside from within the units. Each interior is treated as a simple volume or shell in which the distinct elements of the space can more clearly emerge. Polished-concrete floors create a uniform field condition at the ground plane. Plainly painted drywall walls and an exposed steel truss and metal deck roof system continue the effect of creating a quiet background field in which feature elements can construct spatial and textural complexity.

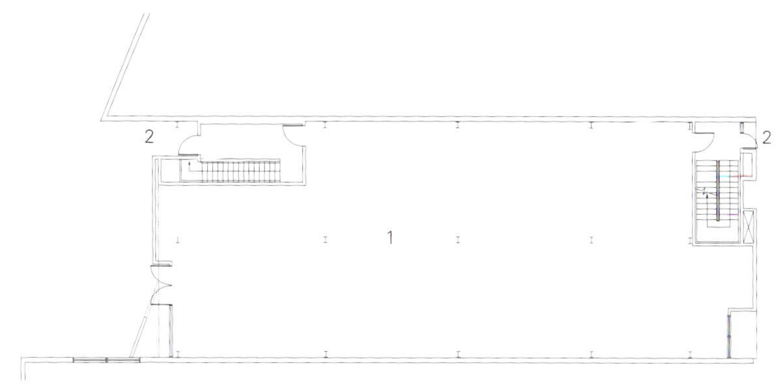

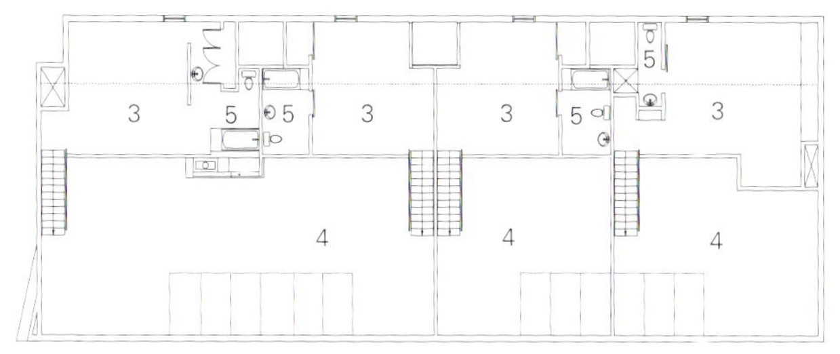

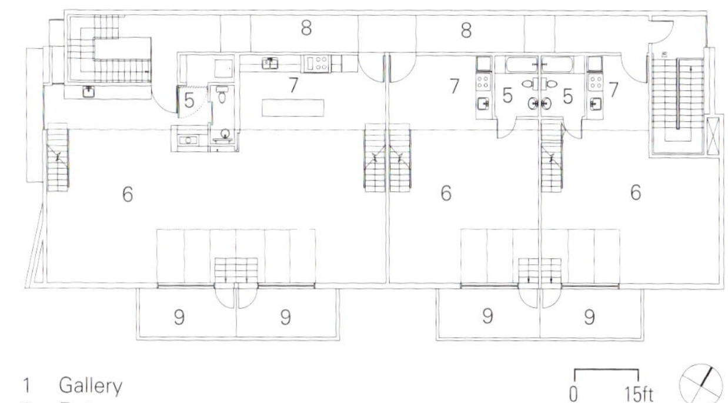

1 Gallery
2 Entrance
3 Loft living area
4 Open to area below
5 Bath
6 Loft live/work space
7 Kitchen
8 Hall
9 Deck

0 15ft

opposite top Generous sunlight floods loft units
opposite bottom Steel decking and bar joists are exposed
left Concrete floors fit artistic aesthetic
top Unit floor plans include gallery space

top left	Elevations are restrained and elegar
left	Interior spaces offer views between levels
opposite top	Section through units
opposite bottom	Deck outside living level
Photography	Marvin Rand and Benny Chan

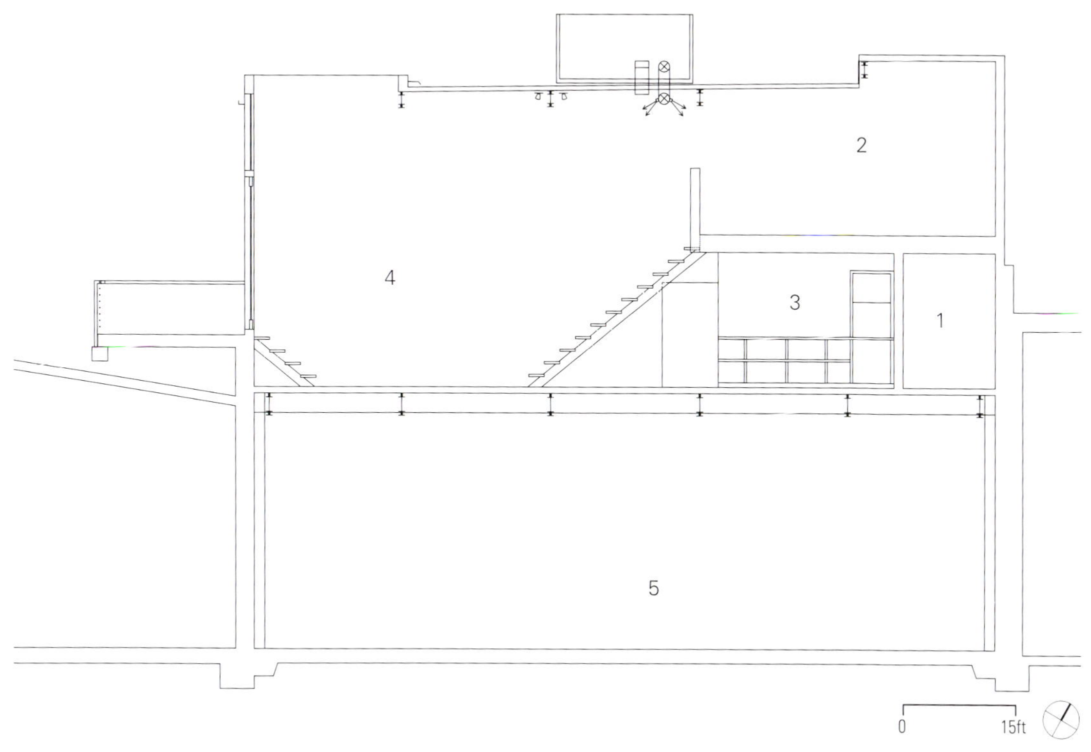

1 Hall
2 Mezzanine
3 Kitchen
4 Living/work space
5 Gallery

Esther Short Commons

Vancouver, Washington, USA

William Wilson Architects

bottom Site plan of complex
opposite All units are accessed from a common entrance

The primary architectural design goals for Esther Short Commons (ESC) respond to the unique location within the city and provide innovative construction details, while contributing to the residents' quality of life.

The neighborhood around Esther Short Commons has been transformed from an edge location for light industry, to a cultural center for downtown Vancouver. ESC contributes to this increasingly vibrant neighborhood by providing affordable downtown living options and convenient access to work and mass transit. In addition, ESC provides safe and enjoyable affordable housing for residents at a variety of income levels. Construction cost was $78 per square foot, including site work.

Increased pedestrian activity adds to the street life around Esther Short Park. Overhead doors connect the farmer's market to the weekend street market. Market vendors include artists, craftspeople, musicians, food venders, flower vendors, coffee shops, and a specialty meat market. Additional retail space includes a family dentist, several restaurants and a home furnishings store.

The site design responds to a number of constraints (limited parking and large internal area) and takes advantage of a number of urban opportunities (views, sunlight and urban location). Each of the 160 apartments has an exterior deck and 82 percent of the units receive direct sunlight. The apartment configuration and decks take full advantage the dramatic bridge and river views. Commercial areas are transparent from the street to interior gardens beyond. This increases light, mitigates the mass of the building, and allows south light to silhouette the gardens. Glass block walls in the lobby and community room also allow diffused light into interior spaces while providing privacy for residents.

Most of the available street frontage is utilized for commercial business; the remainder is used for access to the interior surface parking area. Innovative detailing responds to the wet climate and leverages off-site fabrication, including a deck-railing and screen system, a cornice support structure, and a street awning system. Cantilevered structural decks allow water to shed off three sides and aids the wetting and drying cycle.

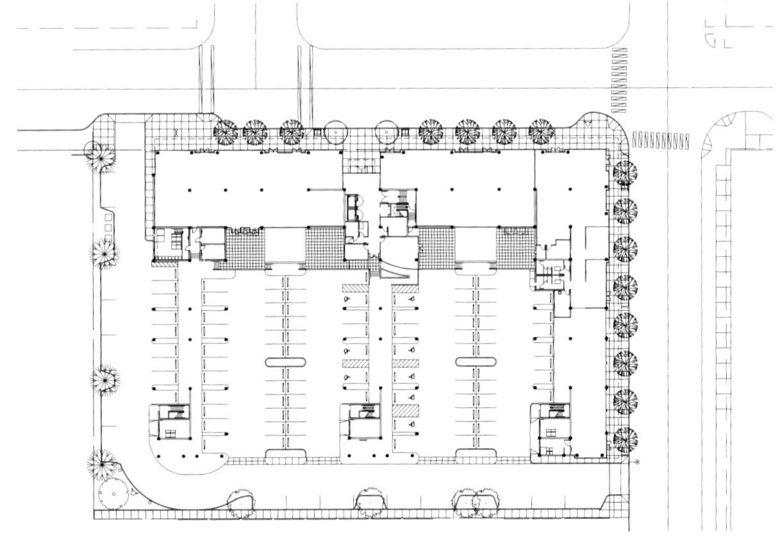

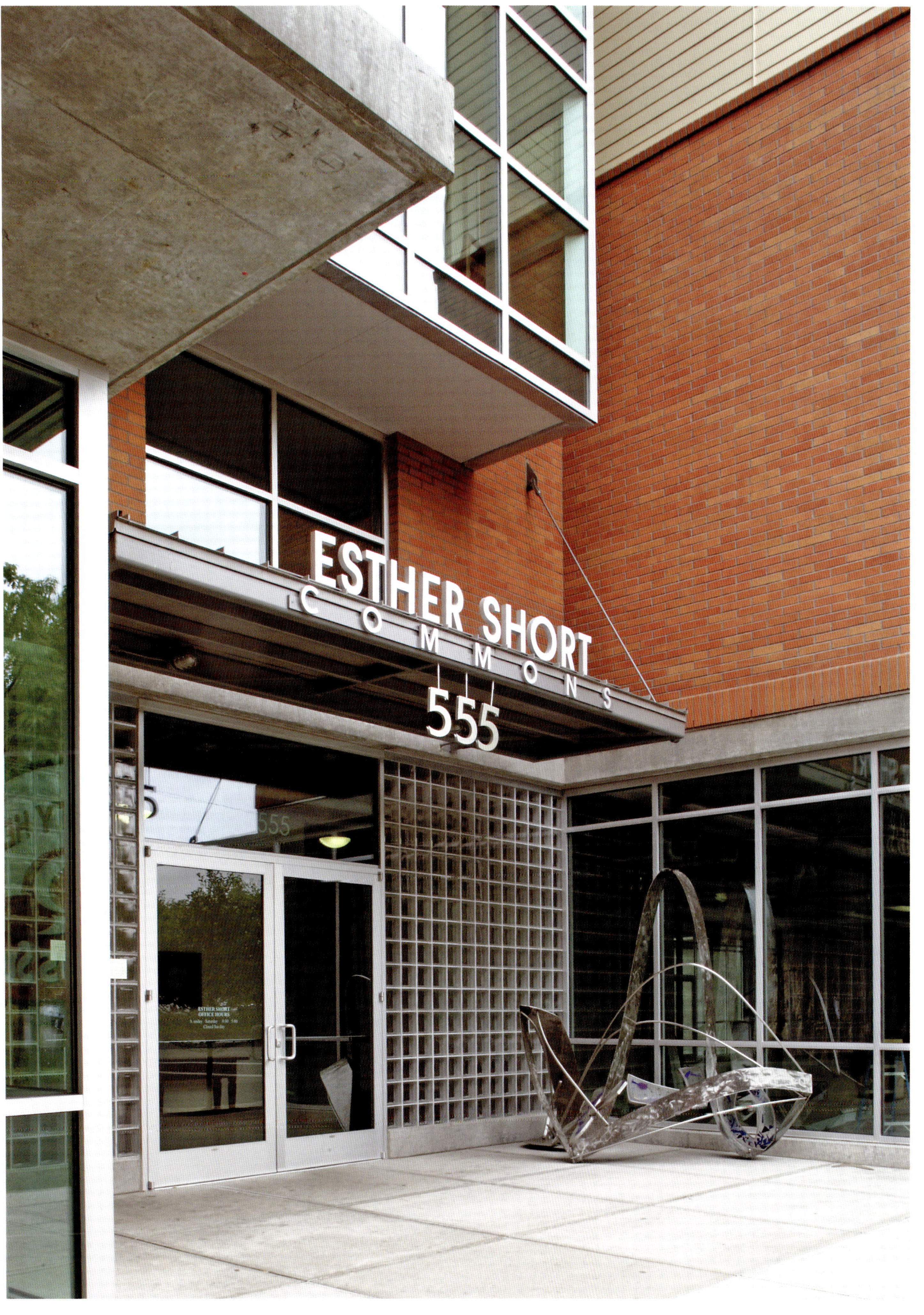
ESTHER SHORT
COMMONS
555

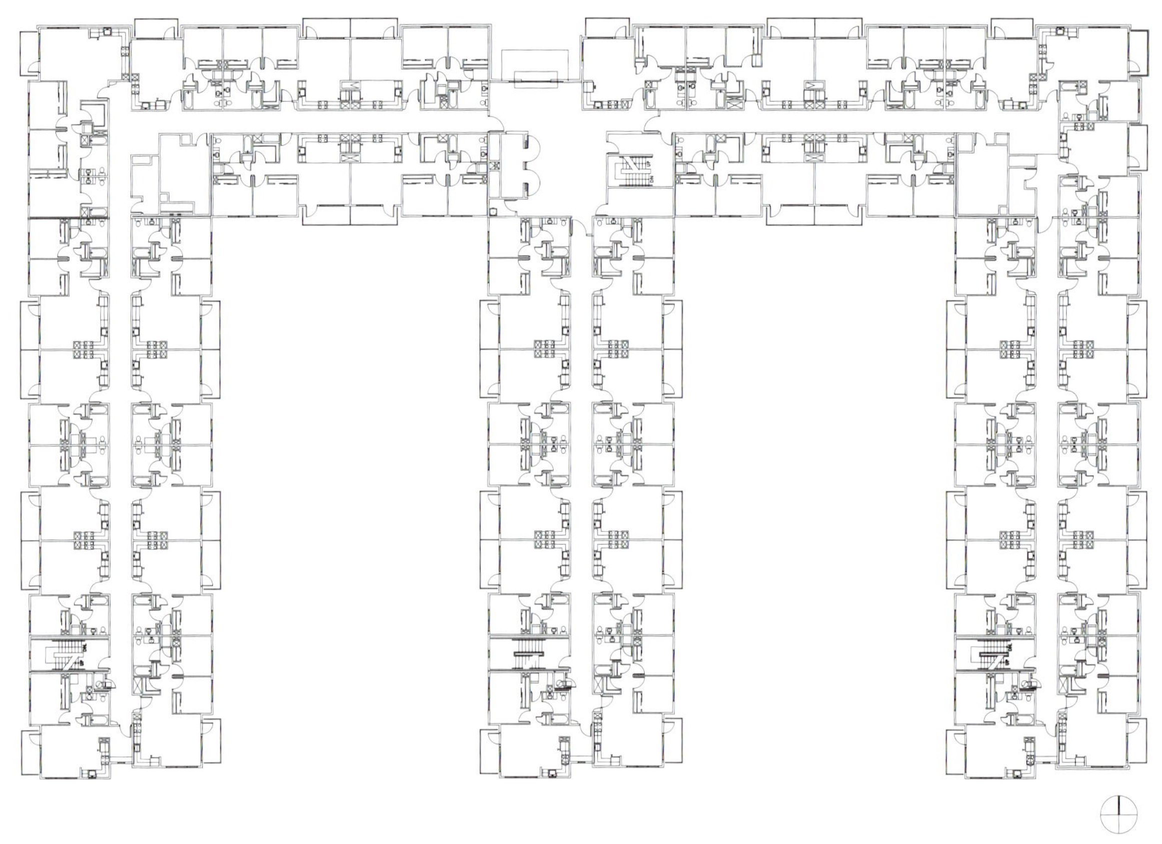

opposite top	Mid-level floor plan
opposite bottom	Balconies for each apartment
below left	Complex establishes a strong street presence
below right	Perforated wall brings in daylight
bottom left	Entrance is found under projecting bay windows
bottom right	Retail is protected under canopies

top Retail space occupies ground level
opposite top Retail spaces open onto outdoor spaces
opposite bottom Complex encourages community activity
Photography Sally Painter

HONEY

cker Orchards
Hood River, Oregon
est 1915

Magnolia Row

West Oakland, California, USA

David Baker + Associates

bottom Magnolia Row in its neighborhood context
opposite Vine-covered trellis marks entry

These townhouse lofts are market-rate for-sale housing located in West Oakland. They provide an entry-level housing opportunity while revitalizing this centrally located historic neighborhood.

This 36-unit project bridges the gap between industrial and residential neighborhoods, with a project density of 30 units per acre. Large windows and low-sloped roofs reflect the aesthetic of the nearby warehouses, while the scale of the buildings, fiber-cement lap-board exterior siding painted in different colors, trellises, and gardens mix well with the area's restored Victorian-era homes. The see-saw pitch of the roofs along Magnolia Street animates the development and gives it a fun-loving atmosphere. Small touches such as delicate trellises over the unit entries, and concrete strips instead of fully paved driveways help to give Magnolia Row its distinctive intimate human scale. All units have one designated parking space.

This project is a hybrid of urban lofts and townhouses. There are 20 loft apartments along Magnolia Street and 16 two-bedroom units along 32nd Street. Both the three-story units along Magnolia and the two-story units on 32nd Street offer large, open loft-style living areas combined with private bedrooms. Living room areas in the Magnolia units are two-story, with bedroom lofts above overlooking the two-story space. Interior materials include hardwood floors, granite countertops, under-mounted sinks, and open-riser stairs with varnished wood treads which help to provide a focal point in the first-floor living area and allows views through the staircase throughout the unit.

The townhouses include energy-efficient hydronic forced-air heat, high-efficiency water heaters, and pre-wiring for home security systems, multiple phone lines, and an Ethernet network.

Clawson Lofts
32nd Street
0
40ft

1202
1200

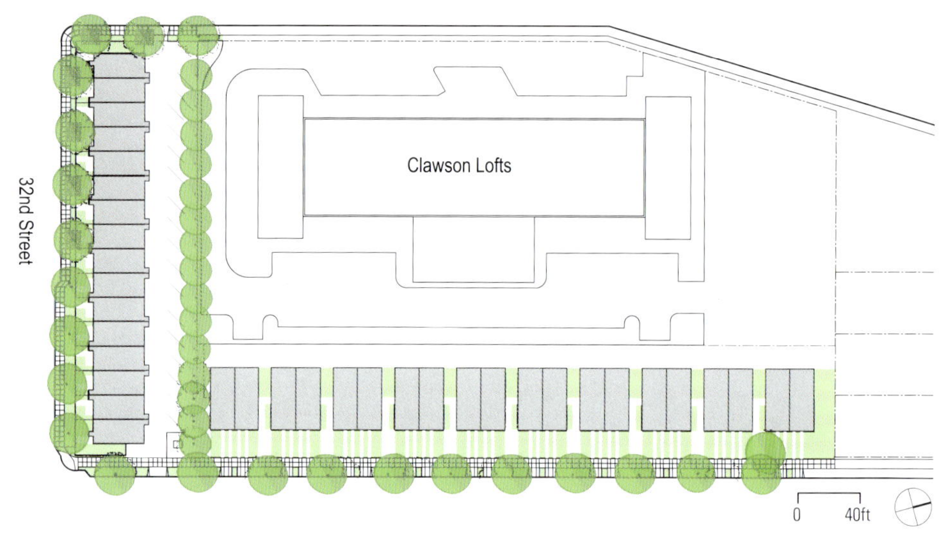

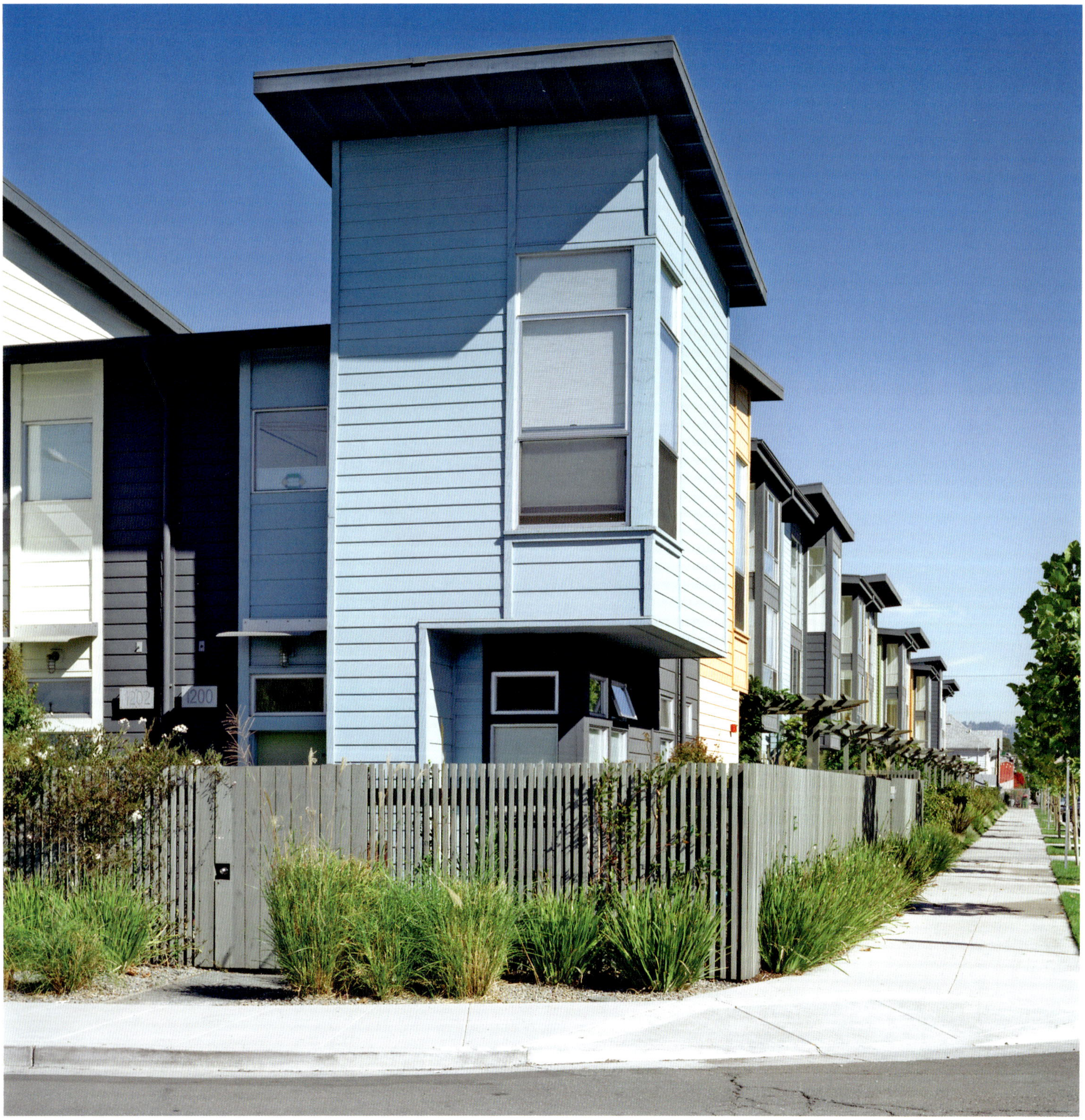

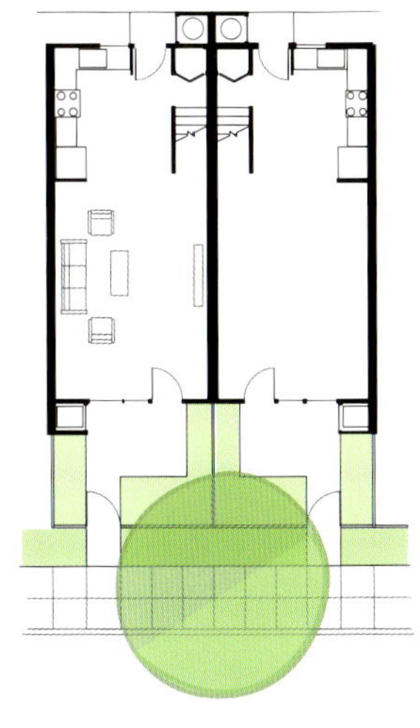

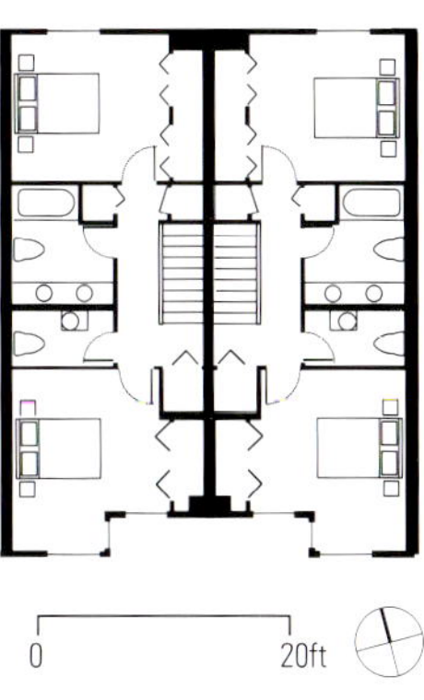

opposite top Unit plans along 32nd Street
opposite bottom Two-story units at street corner
left Second floor plan of 32nd Street units
bottom Three-story units face Magnolia
bottom left Light-filled and colorful interiors
bottom right Open-riser stairs permit views between spaces
Photography David Baker + Partners

Briar Hills

Omaha, Nebraska, USA

Randy Brown Architects

Briar Hills is comprised of three 24-unit apartment buildings with one- and two-bedroom plans, along with a clubhouse, pool, fitness room, and garages. The architect's approach to creating this affordable housing project on a sloping site was to define a community—a small village of buildings organized around a green courtyard that leads to the clubhouse/pool/fitness facilities.

The design goals were straightforward. The architects wanted to avoid the "sameness" of an apartment complex—a common suburban building type that often is not adventurous architecturally. They also wanted to resist the monolithic "flatness" of many such apartment complexes, which are essentially boxes. They stressed natural, expressive materials for siding, fences, windows, decks, trim, and doors. They also wanted to create well-proportioned buildings with inviting entries that serve as transitions from inside to out, providing overhead cover during inclement weather.

Innovative details result in an experience from car to house richly alive with texture, natural color, and beauty. The design of the landscaping is an integral part of the architecture and results in outdoor spaces that possess a visual calmness. Each building is located at a different elevation, stepping down the site. Resultant views from each apartment are staggered so as not to look directly into neighboring apartments, but to private and public outdoor spaces surrounding the complex. Parking is pushed to the periphery of the site so as to preserve the quiet, park-like green space of the site interior, through which people circulate to their individual units.

Exterior materials include synthetic stucco, sheet metal, standing seam siding, clear cedar plywood, and wire mesh. Unit interiors are distinguished by affordable yet sensitive materials such as maple hardwood flooring, stained concrete, and carpeting.

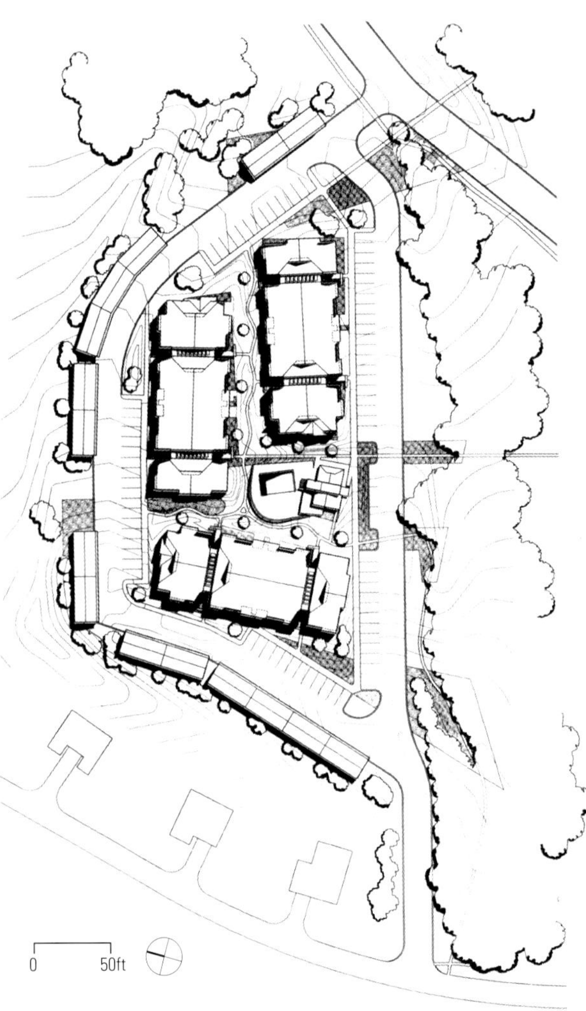

left Site design emphasizes the 'village' character

opposite Stucco, unfinished wood, and wire mesh used on exterior

top The three buildings are organized around a community space
bottom left Plywood is used throughout as a warm material
bottom right Planes of different colors appear to advance and recede
opposite top Wooden balconies play off the stucco finishes
opposite left Section detail of walkway trellis
opposite right Clear cedar plywood wall of rear elevation

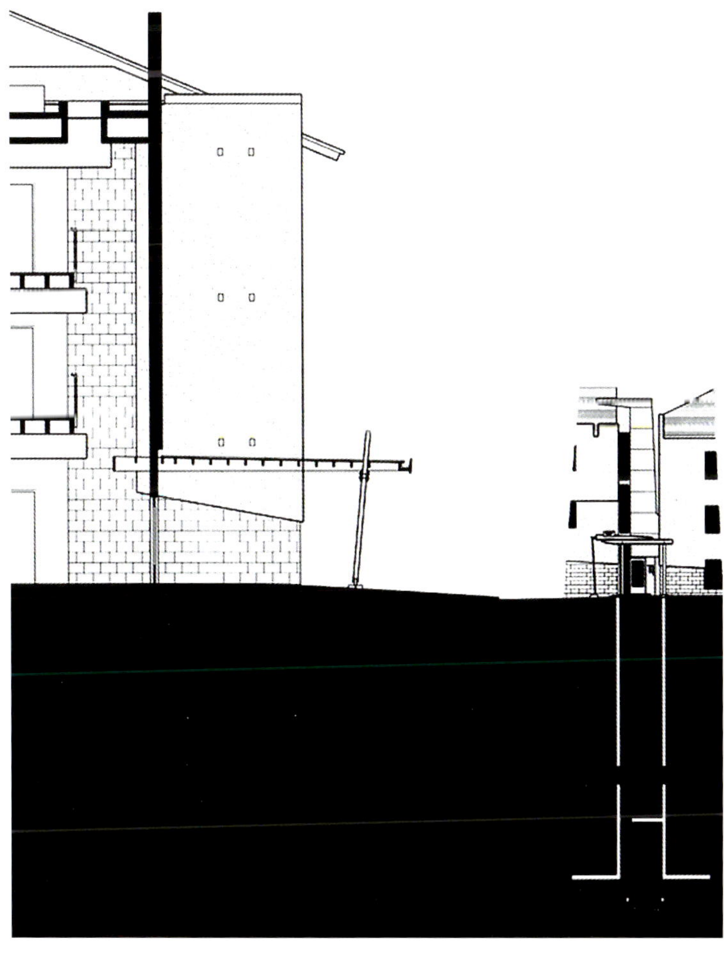

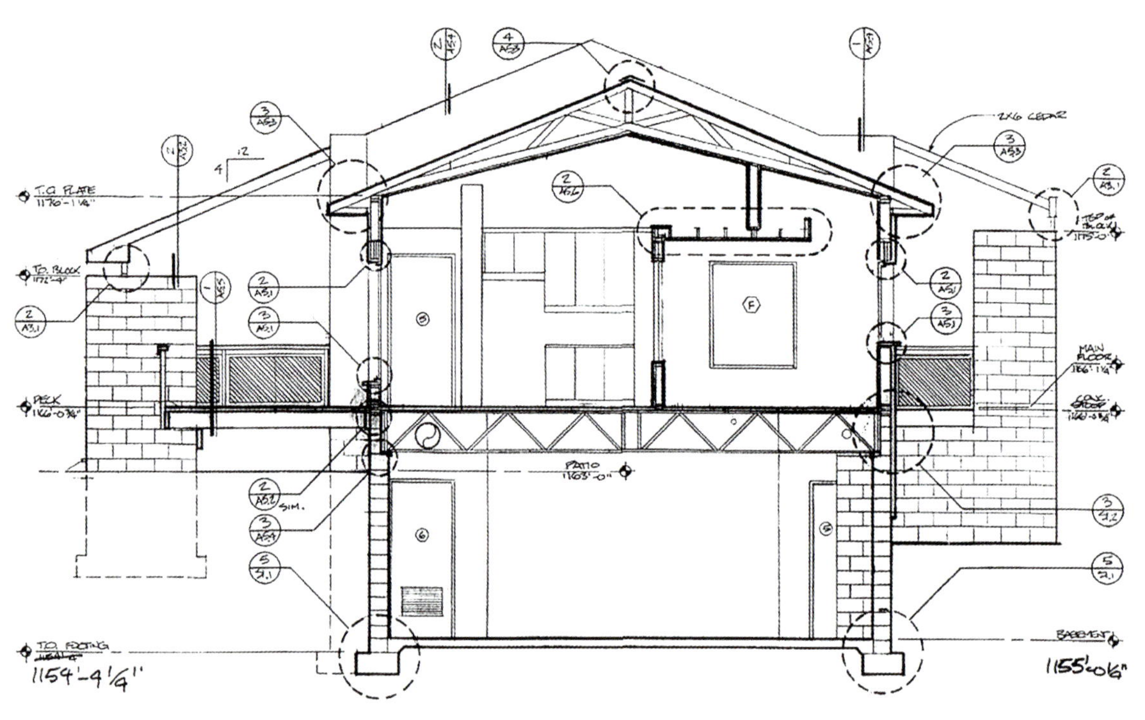

2X6 CEDAR
T.O. PLATE
T.O. BLOCK
DECK
MAIN FLOOR
PATIO
SIM.
T.O. FOOTING
1154'-4 1/4"
BASEMENT
1155'-0 1/8"

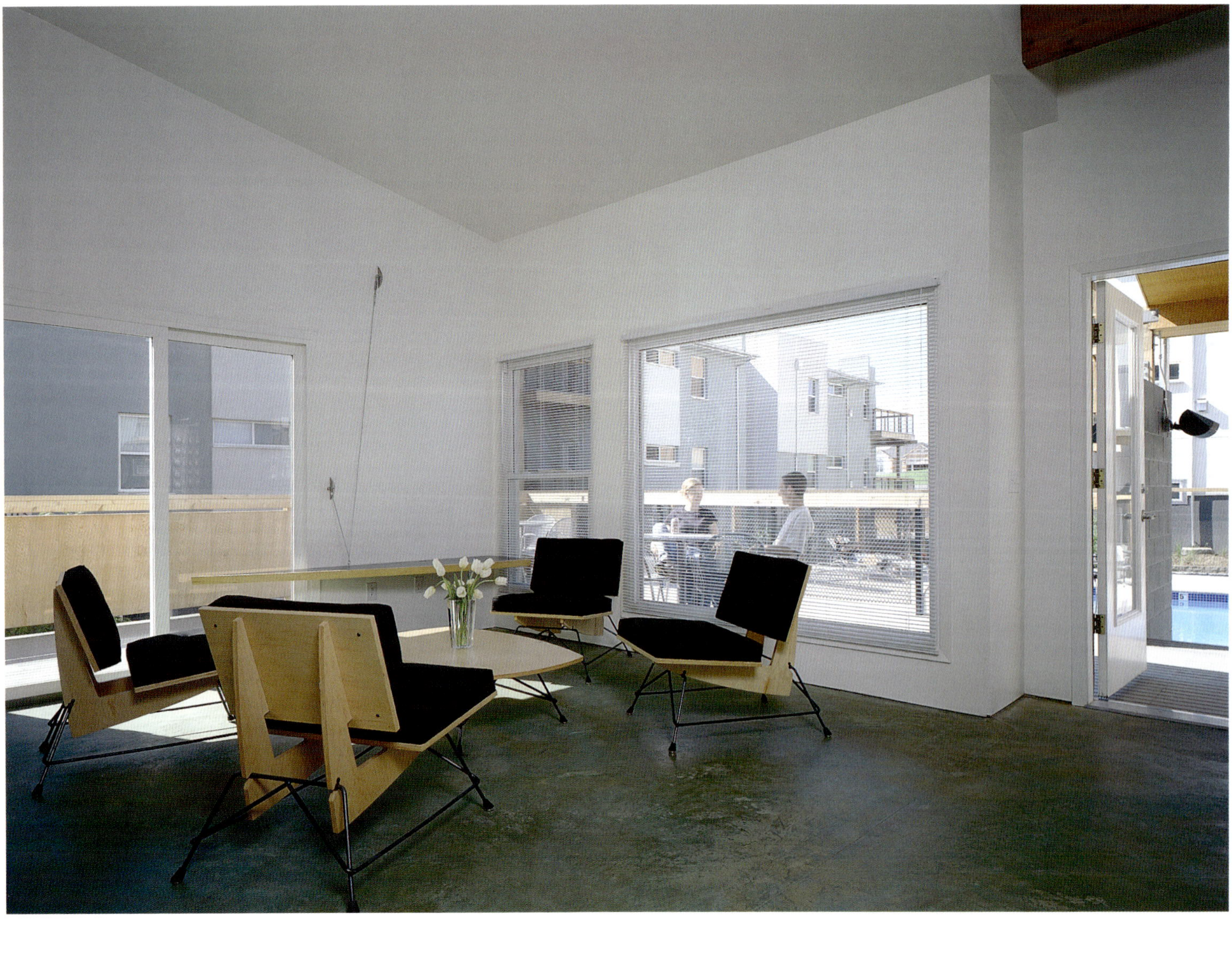

opposite top	Section through one of three apartment buildings
opposite bottom	Views are maximized throughout interior
bottom	Light-colored but affordable materials stress economy
Photography	Farshid Assassi

Harold Way

Los Angeles, California, USA

Koning Eizenberg Architecture

bottom Elevation showing space between apartment blocks
opposite Spaces between blocks encourage ventilation

Providing families with amenity, community, and a quality living environment is the intent of the design for the Harold Way Apartments. Economy is a given and simple stacked planning provided the key to economy. All units are cross-ventilated and have exterior access and balconies or garden space. Access is organized to optimize privacy and orchestrate changes of scale. Consequently, there are stacked three-bedroom, two-level townhouses rather than four levels of three-bedroom flats. The two-bedroom units feature a floor-to-ceiling sliding glass door that allows abundant natural light and ventilation. The creamy stucco wings have simple elevations that rely on proportion and disposition of glazing and balconies for ornament.

The one-bedroom unit blocks step down from four to two stories in the middle of the site and are clad in cement board with wood battens painted a soft shade of gray/green. Vines are intended to eventually cover the walls. These units provide a textural and spatial foil to the formal stucco volumes and loosely describe a courtyard space on one side and a street-like space on the other. In addition to the vines, hedges of bamboo provide a natural vertical accent and screens to the one-bedroom patios at the ground floor.

The community room fills the ground-level southwest entry corner (Western and Harold) as a sign of welcome. Along the heavily traveled Western Boulevard, the elevation is punctuated by private balconies clad in spaced boards made of recycled plastic. Side railings are open vertical steel pickets to allow clearer glances up to the Hollywood Hills, while the fronts of the balconies are more opaque to screen objects that tend to accumulate with occupancy. Soffits of the balconies are a bright green accent. The remainder of the façade is organized by tall portions of lapped-metal siding that divide the elevation into three crisp well-proportioned stucco sections. Ground floor units are screened from the street by a stepped masonry wall clad in flowering vines. Trees are placed along each side of the sidewalk to eventually form a canopy for pedestrians traveling to nearby shops and the subway station a quarter-mile north of the site.

top Section showing cross ventilation through units
top right Perforated blocks permit views and ventilation
right Slatted balconies permit glimpses of views
opposite Block configuration fills out the urban site

top Complex rises from its green/gray base
bottom, left to right Floor plans from ground to upper-level

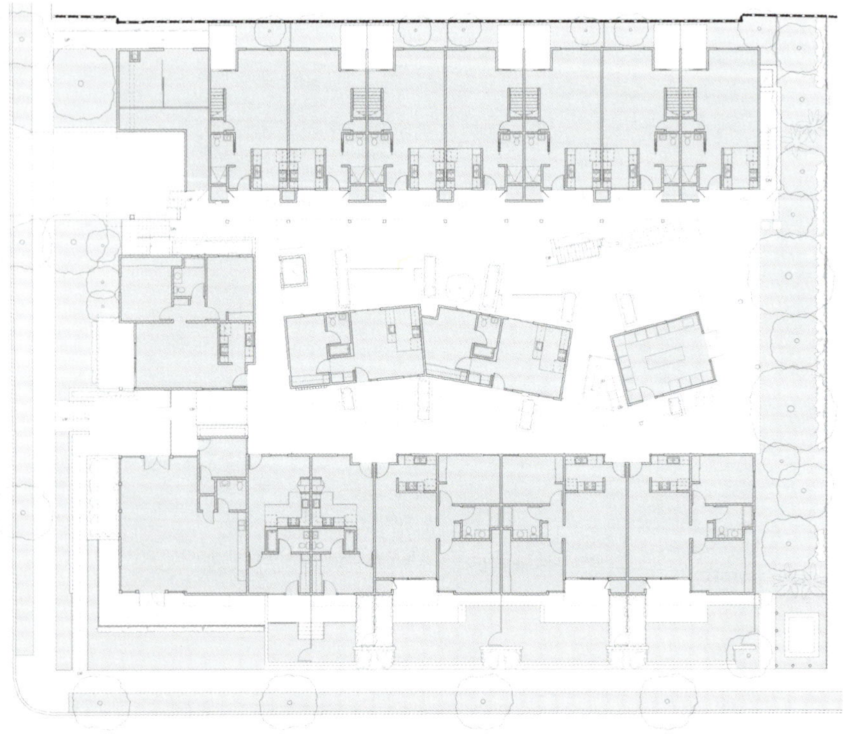

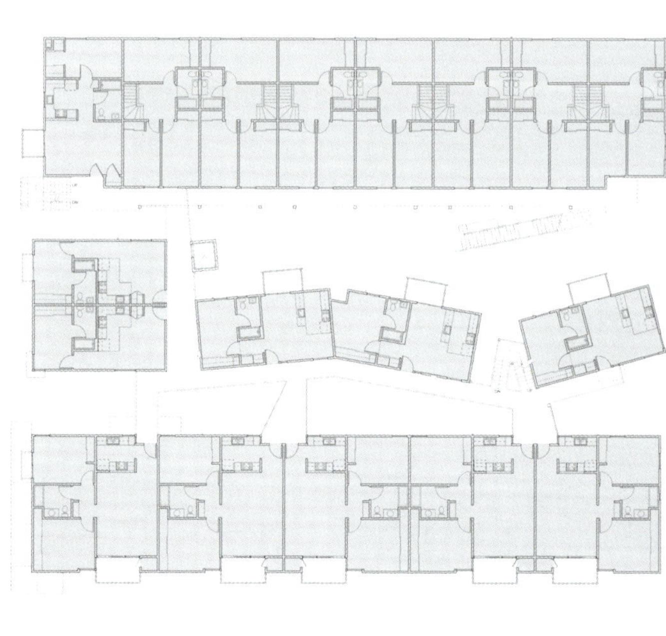

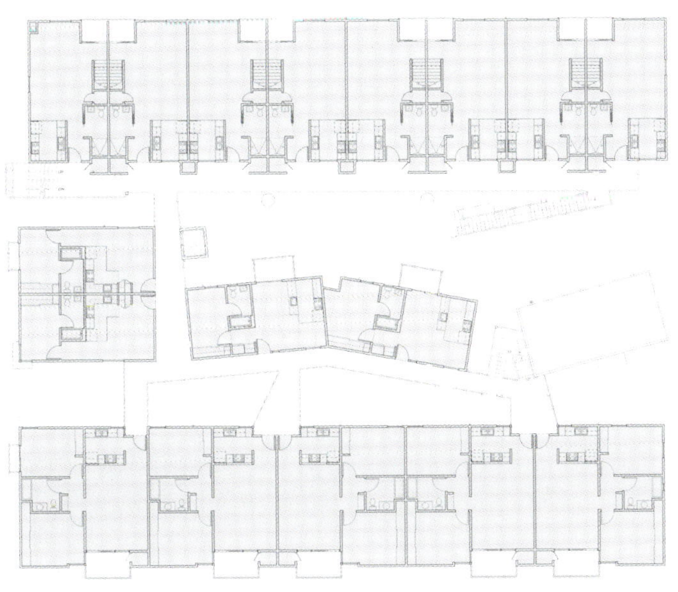

opposite Interior courtyard with circulation weaves throughout interior courtyard
right Overview of courtyard space
far right Stairway provides a sculptural element
bottom Verdant landscaping softens urban edges
Photography Benny Chan

Douglas Meadows

Portland, Oregon, USA

Robertson, Merryman, Barnes Architects

bottom	Site plan of complex
opposite top	Unit buildings have strong residential scale
opposite bottom	A private outdoor space for gathering
Photography	Michael Mathers

Human Solutions, a Community Development Corporation that provides a variety of services to homeless families, developed Douglas Meadows. Nestled into a slim third-of-an-acre rectangular lot, Douglas Meadows creates its own mini-community. A path meanders past the eight two-story, three- or four-bedroom craftsman-style units that range in size from 1232 to 1438 square feet. There are community garden beds, bioswales, and a children's play area. Mature trees, carefully protected during design and construction, shade the site and provide wildlife habitat.

The design focus for this project is energy efficiency and sustainability, in part to improve the affordability of the units by lowering life-cycle and maintenance costs. The rectangular site's longest dimension is east-west, which maximizes solar exposure to the south. In each unit, a single gas water heater provides hot water for washing and a hydronic space-heating system with thermostats in every room. In addition, a small grant from the Office of Sustainable Development and Northwest Natural allowed Human Solutions to upgrade to Energy Star appliances. Other energy-efficient features include: wastewater heat exchangers, compact fluorescent lights, water-conserving showers, tight construction to minimize drafts and air leaks, high-performance windows, overhangs, and insulating window shades.

Along with these energy-conserving items, Douglas Meadows incorporates a number of sustainable or "green" features. Materials with recycled-content were used for playground surfacing, gypsum wall board, fiberglass batt insulation, exterior paint, plastic lumber, steel fence posts, salvaged lumber, and old concrete pavers. Carpeting is made of recycled plastic soda bottles. Landscape architect Gretchen Vadnais created a water-conserving and edible "permaculture" landscape. In a few years, the apple trees, kiwi vines, blueberry bushes will bear their fresh, flavorful and money-saving harvest for residents of the Douglas Meadows community.

Construction cost for the project was $800,000, which works out to $84 per square foot.

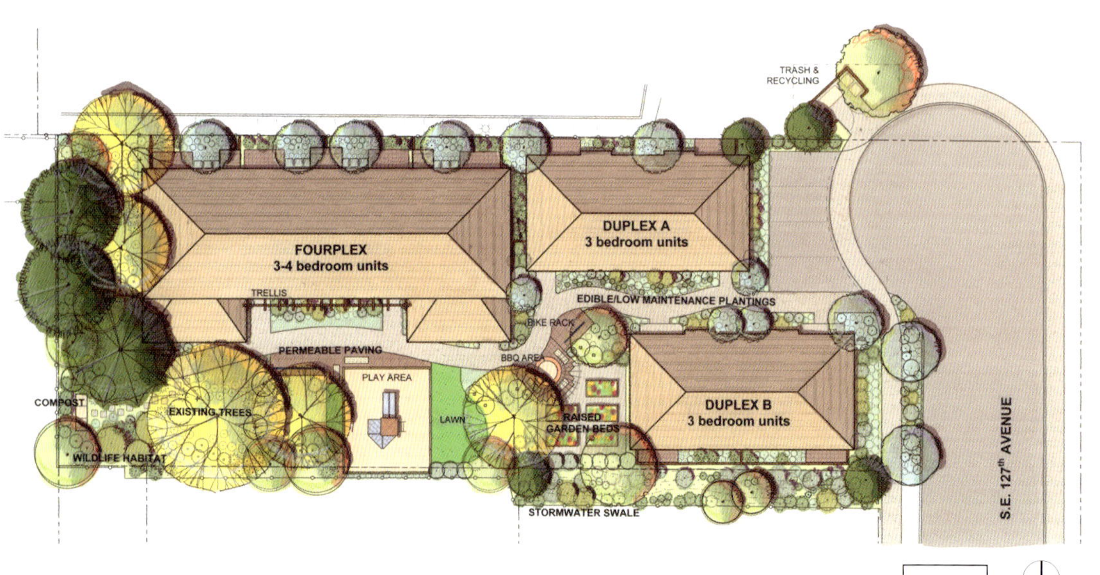

5-8

Bentley-
Massachusetts

Los Angeles, California, USA

Kanner Architects

Living up to the example of a master of modern architecture was the main design challenge when Kanner Architects began the Bentley-Massachusetts Apartments in Los Angeles's Westwood neighborhood. Two apartment buildings designed by Richard Neutra stand in the same neighborhood. The Landfair and Strathmore Westwood apartment buildings, both opened in 1937, illustrate Neutra's design approach of taking advantage of Southern California's bright light and plentiful breezes. Neutra set out to smash the distinction between inside and outside.

Bentley-Massachusetts employs large expanses of glass, fourth-floor terraces and wide, street-facing balconies to bring light and fresh air into spacious units. The base of the four-story project is cantilevered and set back to acknowledge the pedestrian character of the neighborhood. The cantilever also gives the project a sense of lightness as the main body of the form sits above its recessed base. The owner/builders live on the fourth level and agreed to set back this level as well. That decision resulted in wide terraces that reinforced the façade's horizontal composition.

The first three levels of the building comprise 11 two-bedroom units. The fourth floor has two, three-bedroom penthouses. All floor plans are spacious, with nine-foot ceilings and open plans for the kitchen, dining and living rooms.

The building has two personas: its daytime presence is that of a white ocean liner—horizontal and streamlined, filled with joy and optimism. At night it takes on a more romantic lantern-like quality where the figure/ground of the solid plaster fascias and transparent expanses of glass reverse intensities. Warm incandescent light spills out onto the street adding a festive quality to the neighborhood.

Smooth plaster, mosaic tile and a clear anodized commercial window system make up a restrained material palette. The landscaping is minimalist and modern and harmonizes with the simplicity of the adjacent structure.

bottom Modernist design was inspired by Neutra
opposite Recessed top and ground floor create interest

top Ground, middle, and penthouse plans
bottom White planes contrast with glass surfaces
opposite Light adds a sense of density to interiors

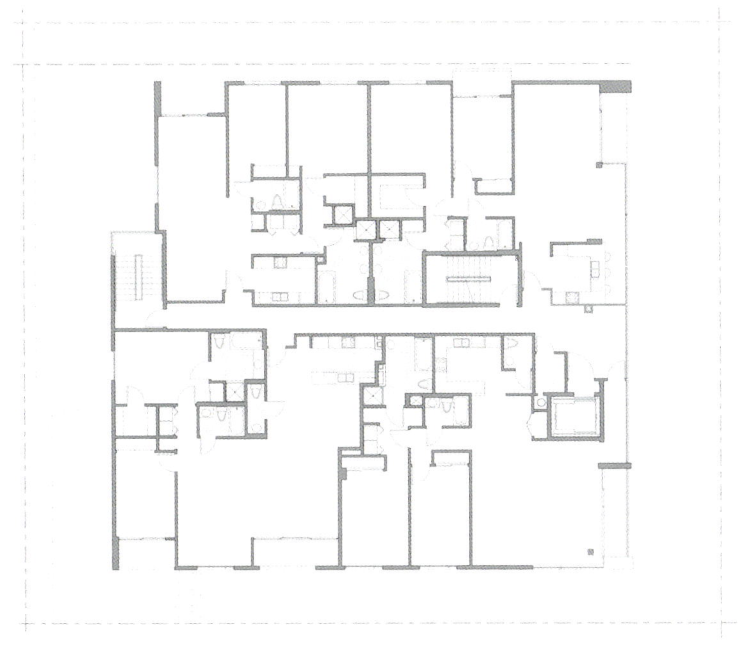

0 20ft

opposite top	Glass corners maximize views
opposite bottom	Interiors are a play of white planes
top	Minimalist design relates to neighboring modern landmarks
Photography	John Edward Linden

18 Yorkville

Toronto, Ontario, Canada

architectsAlliance

This ensemble of buildings, organized around a new public park, has transformed an overlooked stretch of Yonge Street in Toronto, instilling it with an excitement and intensity that reflects its role as the northern gateway to the city's most prestigious retail precinct.

The ensemble consists of 18 Yorkville, a slender, 36-story tower anchored by a seven-story podium that addresses the intersection of Yonge and Yorkville; The Villas at 18 Yorkville, a seven-story townhouse building facing onto a residential side street; and Town Hall Square, a new public park sheltered in the "L" formed by 18 Yorkville and The Villas.

Critical height and density issues were the subject of extensive negotiations with the city's planning and urban design departments, and with local resident and business groups. The result is a beautiful and highly amenable residential complex, which supports the city's master plan objective of intensifying residential and commercial development along key city streets.

From the outset, 18 Yorkville was conceived as the gateway to the historic Village of Yorkville. However, the project was designed with a modernist sensibility. The slender, translucent tower serves as a beacon to mark the entry to the downtown core, and street-level retail and commercial uses in the tower podium reflect the vibrancy of Yonge Street. The grade-related entrances of The Villas fit seamlessly into the Victorian architectural context on Scollard Street. The new public park ties the community together, and enhances the realm of the historic Yorkville Public Library to the west of the site.

bottom Site plan showing tower and townhouses
opposite Tower announces Yorkville Village

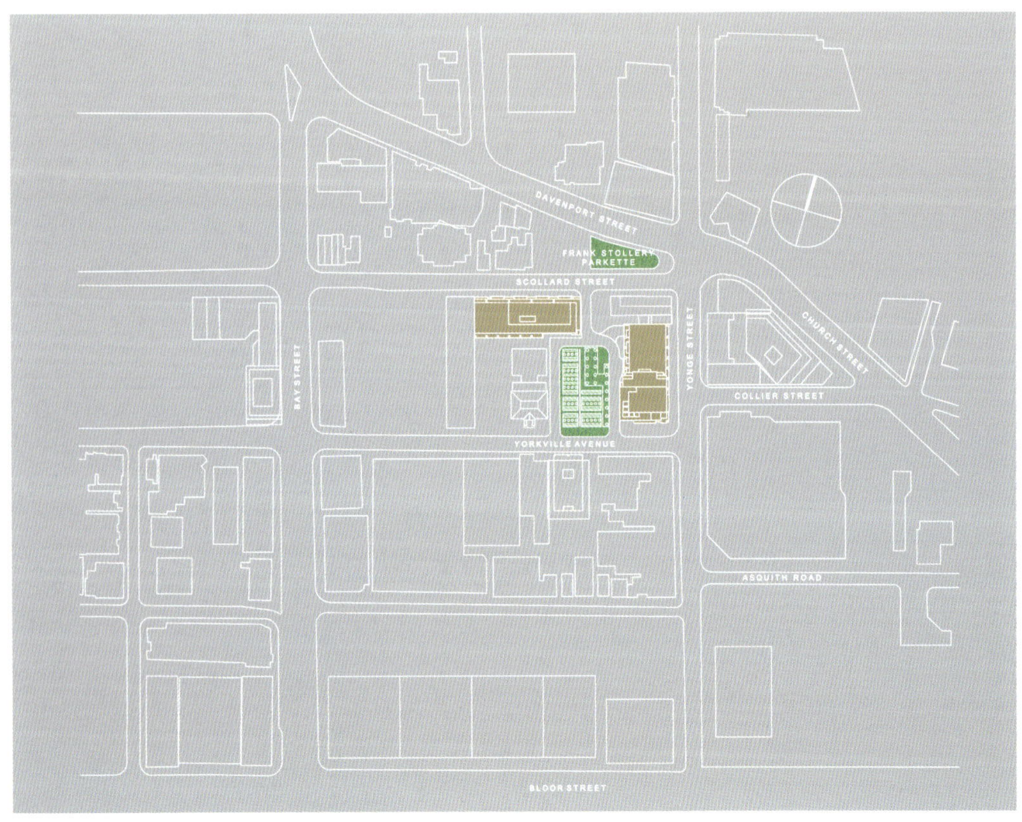

opposite Tower in foreground with nearby villas
top left Tower intensifies urban development in Toronto
top right Balconies articulate the tower's surface
bottom Tower and low-rise residential help define Town Hall Square
Photography A-Frame/Ben Rahn

Lenzen
Square

San Jose, California, USA

David Baker + Partners

bottom	Central entry stair with lattice screen
opposite top left	Complex surrounds a central courtyard
opposite top right	Plan of U-shaped building
opposite bottom	'Green' stair is behind horizontal lattice
Photography	David Baker + Partners

This project is affordable housing geared towards teachers and is located on the edge of an industrial warehouse neighborhood. The project is across the street from the San Jose Unified School District office, which makes it an ideal complex for a teacher on a starting salary. Twenty percent of the units rent at 50 percent of the area's median income, and 80 percent of the units rent at 60 percent of the area's median income.

This project is conveniently located near merchants and restaurants, with access to major freeways. Providing affordable housing in such an ideal location allows residents to live close to work and school, in addition to raising property values and bringing stability to the neighborhood.

The project contains 88 studios, one- and two-bedroom units within two stories above a single-level enclosed parking garage. The U-shaped building defines an at-grade courtyard, which includes a community room, fitness center, computer lab, conference room, generous sized pool, and a children's play area. The units are arranged throughout the three-story complex to overlook the courtyard and survey the surrounding neighborhood.

The form of Lenzen Square is variegated to break down the scale of the project. A central entry stair is located at the base of the U, behind a horizontal lattice screen. The staircase is known as the "green" square, because like a town green it is the place where many residents pass through. Residents then circulate along open-air balcony corridors on the courtyard side of the project to their individual units. Bedrooms poke out along the elevations and are distinguished with seemingly free-standing walls of different colors, with balconies to either side of the walls.

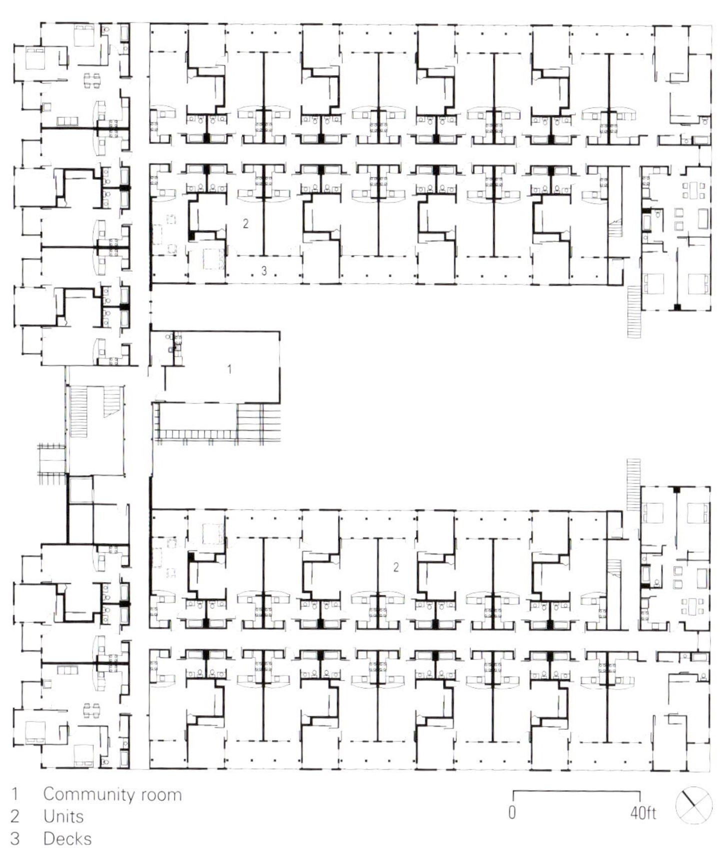
1
2
3
0
40ft
1 Community room
2 Units
3 Decks

Main Street
North

Boulder, Colorado, USA

Wolff Lyon Architects

The 14 residences at Main Street North are part of a mixed-use development that consists of 38,000 square feet of personal service, office, and residential uses on two half-blocks that create the main entrance to a new 330-home neighborhood. The residences are located above office space along the new main street, as well as in free-standing buildings fronting a side street.

Main Street North embodies the traditional values of thoughtful design and good place making by emphasizing that the spaces that buildings create are more important than the buildings themselves. Residents and neighbors feel comfortable moving through or gathering in sun-filled courtyards or private porches. Substantial and timeless building materials are employed in ways that reflect the traditions of the city and region.

The predominantly flat-roofed building forms are a tie to traditional main streets, as are the brick and stone materials used on two of the six buildings. Large storefront windows provide transparency into the shops and bright but varied colorful awnings create additional pedestrian interest at street level. Other window openings are "punched" individually into the building façades in a traditional way and surrounded with enough trim structure to make each feel substantial. Main level entries are recessed into alcoves or placed under arcades to protect them from the elements, giving them greater identity.

In response to the local climate with abundant winter sunshine, all the upper-level units have a covered terrace with most of them facing south. Addressing this concern also results in the façades of the two mixed-use buildings being very different in character. Many of the residences have dramatic high ceilings over their living rooms that open to the sun and view. Contemporary metal sunshades help contribute to the buildings' character and protect their windows.

The six buildings relate to each another to shape the space between them and the outdoor room of the street. Parking needs are well accommodated but without compromising the human scale and vitality of the place.

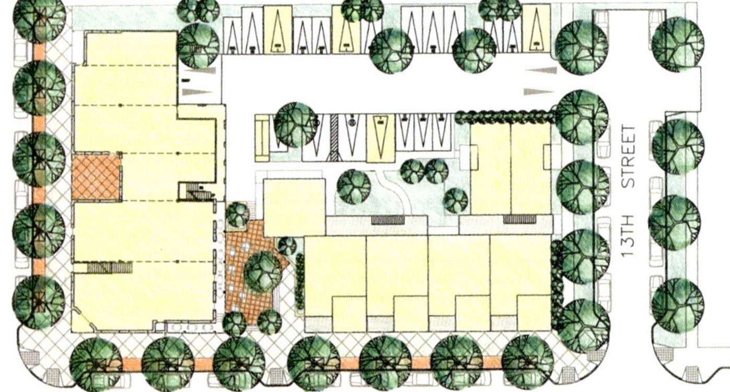

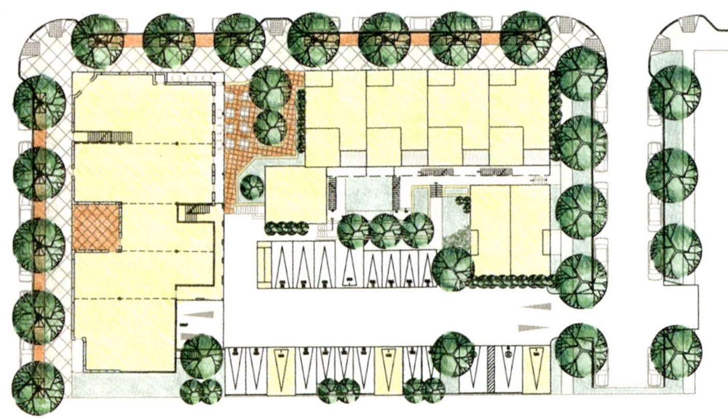

opposite Site plan of two-block development
top Units express the rhythm of the street
bottom left Building forms have a relaxed character
bottom right Units have semi-private outdoor spaces

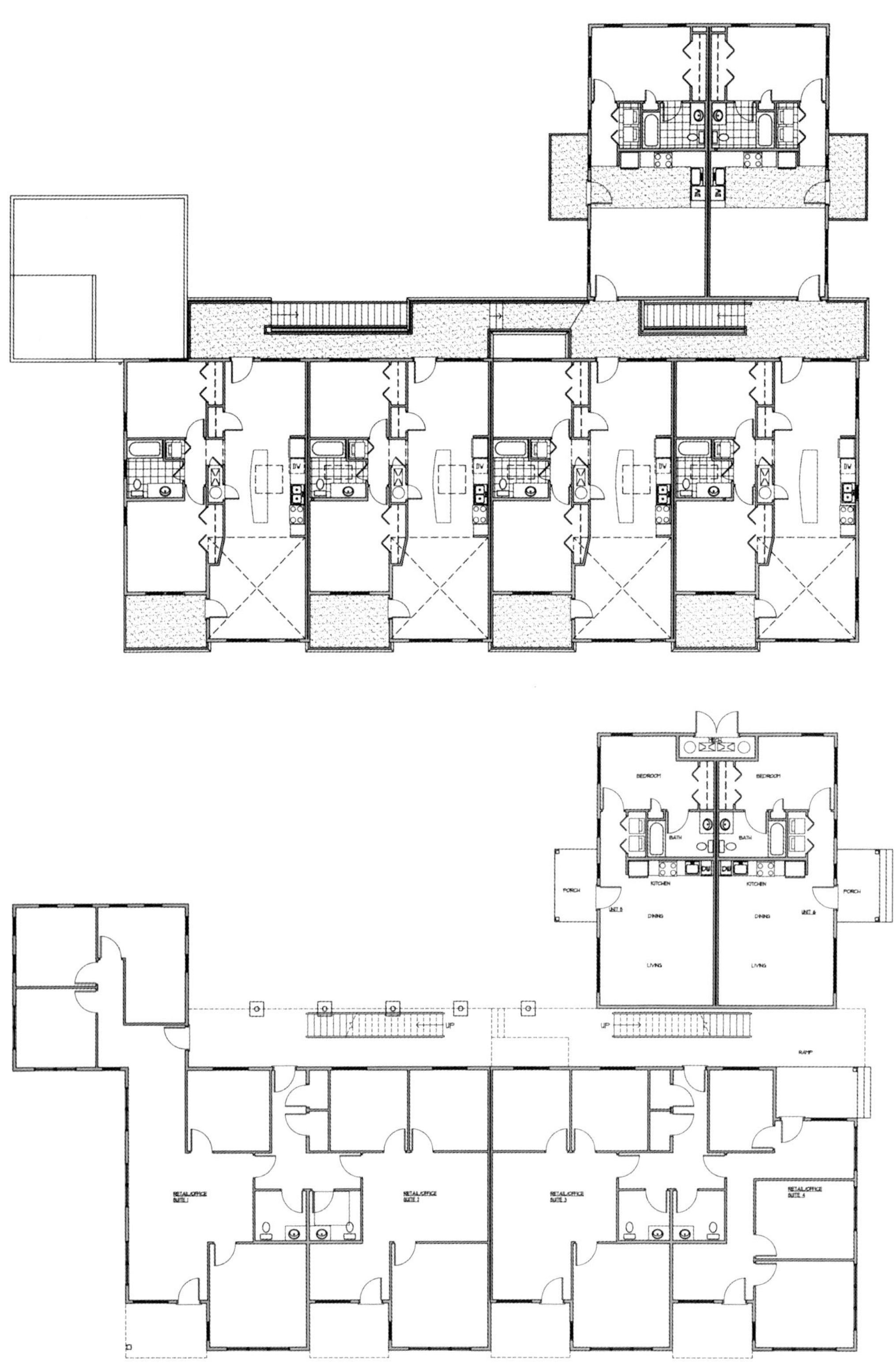

top Upper level plan
above Ground level plan
opposite left Large windows maximize light and views
opposite right Metal sunshades protect windows and cut glare
opposite bottom Kitchens open to living areas
Photography John Wolff

San Pedro Commons

Colma, California, USA

Seidel Holzman

bottom Site plan is organized around a central courtyard
opposite South-facing entry to complex

San Pedro Commons provides 74 affordable residences for seniors in a location conveniently accessible to numerous transit options as well as a walkable pedestrian precinct with ample shopping and services.

The form of the building is clearly derived from the triangular configuration of the site. The necessary angularity of the plan is also carried through into the elevations and massing of the building. The site, pieced together from various remnant parcels, has limited access from the south end and is flanked by a BART transit right-of-way to the west. Despite these encroachments, the project develops a sense of community through the use of a courtyard at the center of the triangular building that brings in light and views.

Various resident amenities are arrayed around the courtyard, including lounges, a library, a senior services office, and meeting rooms. Single-loaded corridors on each of the four floors are arranged to flood the interior with natural light while also providing views into the protected space of the courtyard.

Special consideration was given to maximizing opportunities for San Pedro Commons residents to circulate around the project, thereby encouraging them to walk and socialize within the community. The interior circulation system is a loop that is frequently punctuated by natural light, views, and resident amenities. Likewise, there is an exterior pedestrian loop that circumnavigates the project while providing access to streets that lead to the shopping district and the Colma multi-modal transit station. Stucco, concrete, and metal cladding are the project's predominant materials.

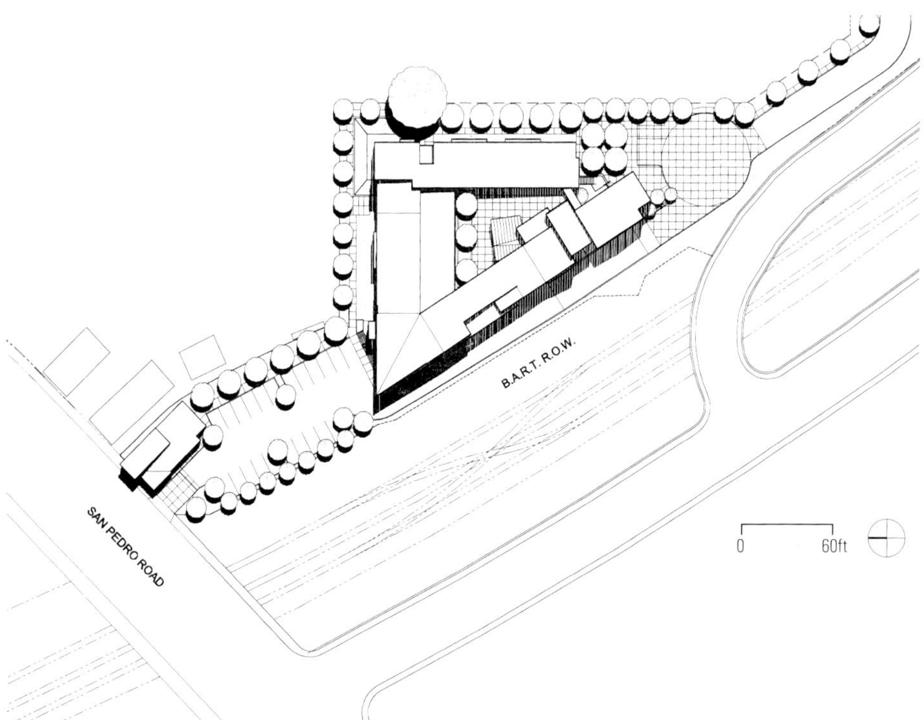

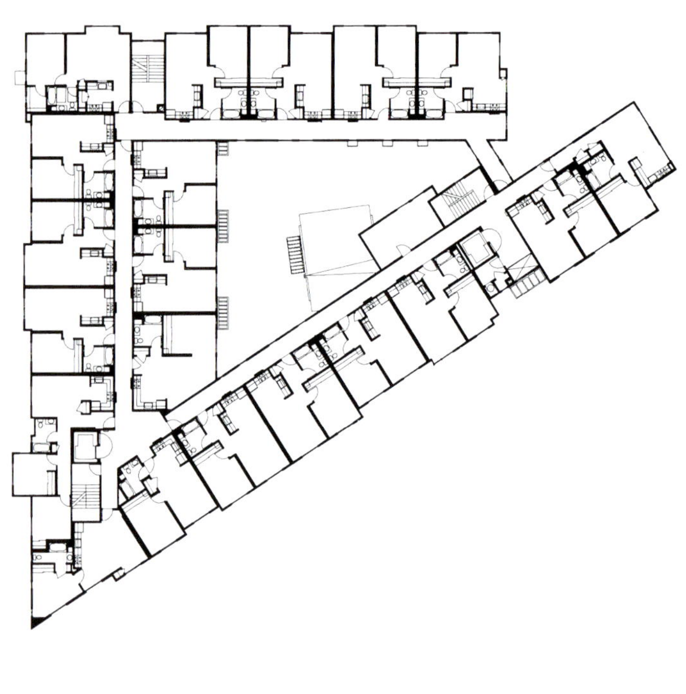

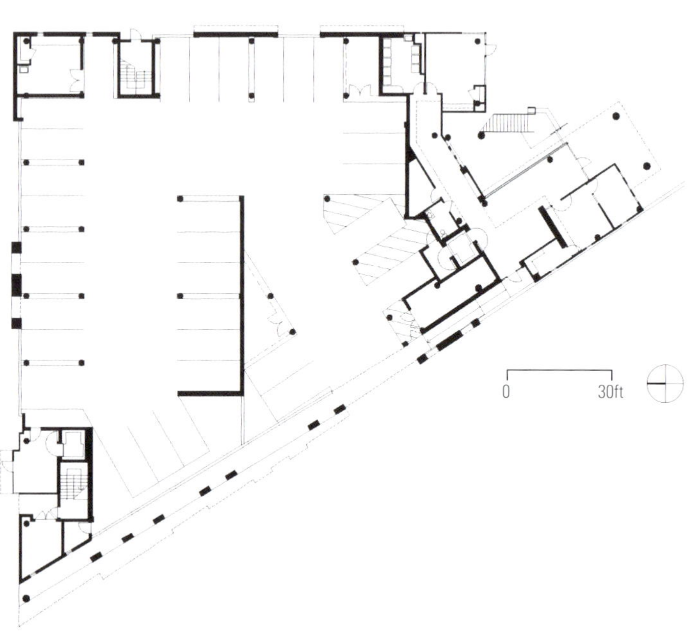
0
30ft

left, top to bottom Upper-floor plan, second-floor plan, ground-floor plan
top Bay windows and setbacks provide variety
far left Interior of courtyard with stair
left Complex as it faces BART right-of-way
Photography Russell Abraham

Wentworth Commons

Chicago, Illinois, USA

Harley Ellis Devereaux

bottom Site plan, with parking to left
opposite Building is surmounted by photovoltaic array

Wentworth Commons, multi-family housing in the Roseland community on Chicago's far south side, is a model for sustainable design strategies and an inspirational cornerstone for its neighborhood. Designed for Mercy Housing Lakefront, a non-profit developer of affordable housing, Wentworth Commons emphasizes socially responsible architecture. It is sustainable in terms of its physical construction and its positive impact on the quality of the lives of its residents, and the social and economic development of its neighborhood.

The Wentworth Commons residence includes 51 affordable apartments ranging in size from one-room efficiency dwellings to four-bedroom units as well as community space and laundry facilities. Supportive services on the ground floor include a family resource center with areas for case management, employment training and leadership development. The federally subsidized project provides housing for low-income families and individuals formerly homeless or at risk of homelessness, with rent based on income.

The four-story masonry building is located on a .77-acre site that bridges business and residential areas. The L-shaped plan holds the corner at a main intersection while providing a secure, sheltered backyard. A collection of homes and a "community within a community," Wentworth Commons blends unit-types together instead of segregating studios from family apartments. The 65,800-square-foot structure is an aggregation of forms expressed in earth-toned exterior masonry. The liveliness of the building's façades reflects diversity and individuality, and helps break down the large scale of elevations over two hundred feet in length. A palette including terracotta, cream, and brick red complements the glazed accent masonry used prominently in the center and at the corners.

The architecture celebrates its sustainability most notably in the exposed roof trusses, which support a photovoltaic system, the use of earth tones exterior masonry, and in interior materials and finishes. The innovative application of sustainable technologies and a "green" design approach to multi-family affordable housing includes energy-efficient strategies, native landscaping including rain gardens and bio-swales to reduce water usage and storm water run-off, and the specification of regional and rapidly renewable materials and finishes.

1 Resident backyard
2 Loading
3 Yard for future program
4 Bioswale/rain garden high point
5 Bioswale/rain garden low point
6 Resident entry
7 Future program entry

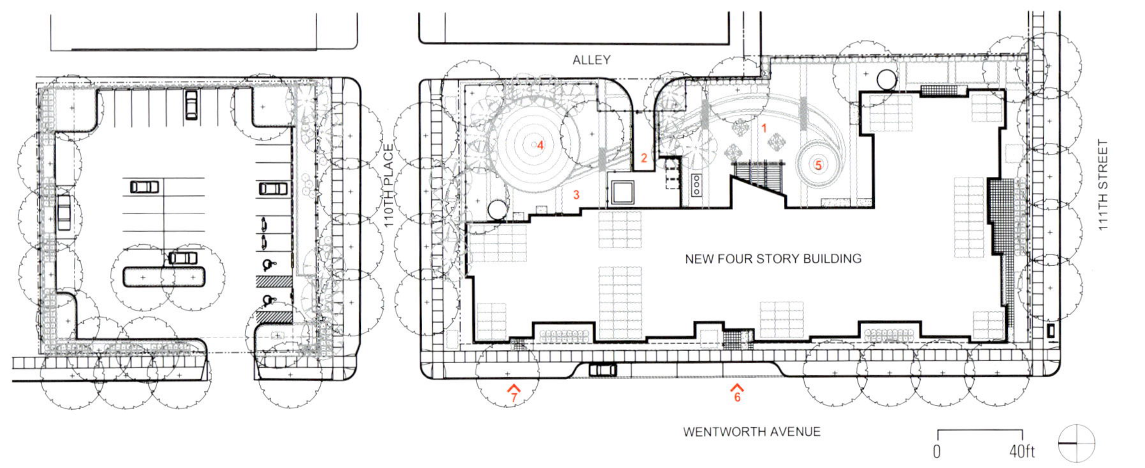

top Typical floor plan
bottom left Shared living room overlooks neighborhood
bottom Development from Wentworth and 111th Street
right Spacious eat-in kitchen with breakfast bar

top Shared lounge near elevator
top right Fourth floor shared living room with glass wall
bottom Photovoltaic arrays visible from Wentworth Avenue
opposite Secondary Wentworth Avenue entrance
Photography Anthony May

more than a roof

Venice Beach
Lofts

Venice, California, USA

Steven Ehrlich Architects

bottom Lofts occupy their tight beach site
Photography Tim Brown
opposite Interiors have an open, utilitarian quality
Photography Elon Shoenholtz

Four lofts occupy this tight 60-x-120-foot site, a half block from the popular and crowded Venice boardwalk. The design maximizes the potential of the small lot and explores how large volumes can extend into the ocean breeze environment. By working within the tight constraints of the lot and a 30-foot height limit, the design allows four beachside units, each at 1900 square feet, to have abundant light, large spaces, balconies, and roof terraces to enhance a relaxed loft-type environment.

A large glass roll-up door allows the principal ground floor gathering space's barrier between indoors and out to evaporate.

A stacked-steel stairway provides vertical circulation from basement parking up through two floors and on to the roof terrace. Parking is a key need; each unit has two spaces in a common concrete semi-subterranean garage that establishes the platform upon which the lofts are constructed.

The lofts' durable, low-maintenance materials are appropriate to the gritty, eclectic Venice neighborhood. The building's exterior of painted vertically corrugated sheet steel contrasts with horizontal planes of galvanized steel. Grey-green stucco wraps the service elements of the project, such as circulation and bathrooms. The interior tectonics are revealed through industrial mechanical ducts, electrical conduits, open wood beams that support the second floor, and exposed, clear-sealed steel moment frames. Additional interior materials express their direct connection to space and materiality—simple, durable, and a further expression of the structural materials.

The concrete main floor serves as the structural deck above the garage. The open beams of the second floor are expressed wood. Fenestration facing the beach is framed in moment frame structural steel expressed both inside and out. Bridges and stairs of steel channels have open steel floor gratings and stainless-steel cable railings. This allows the most minimal intervention of these elements into the space.

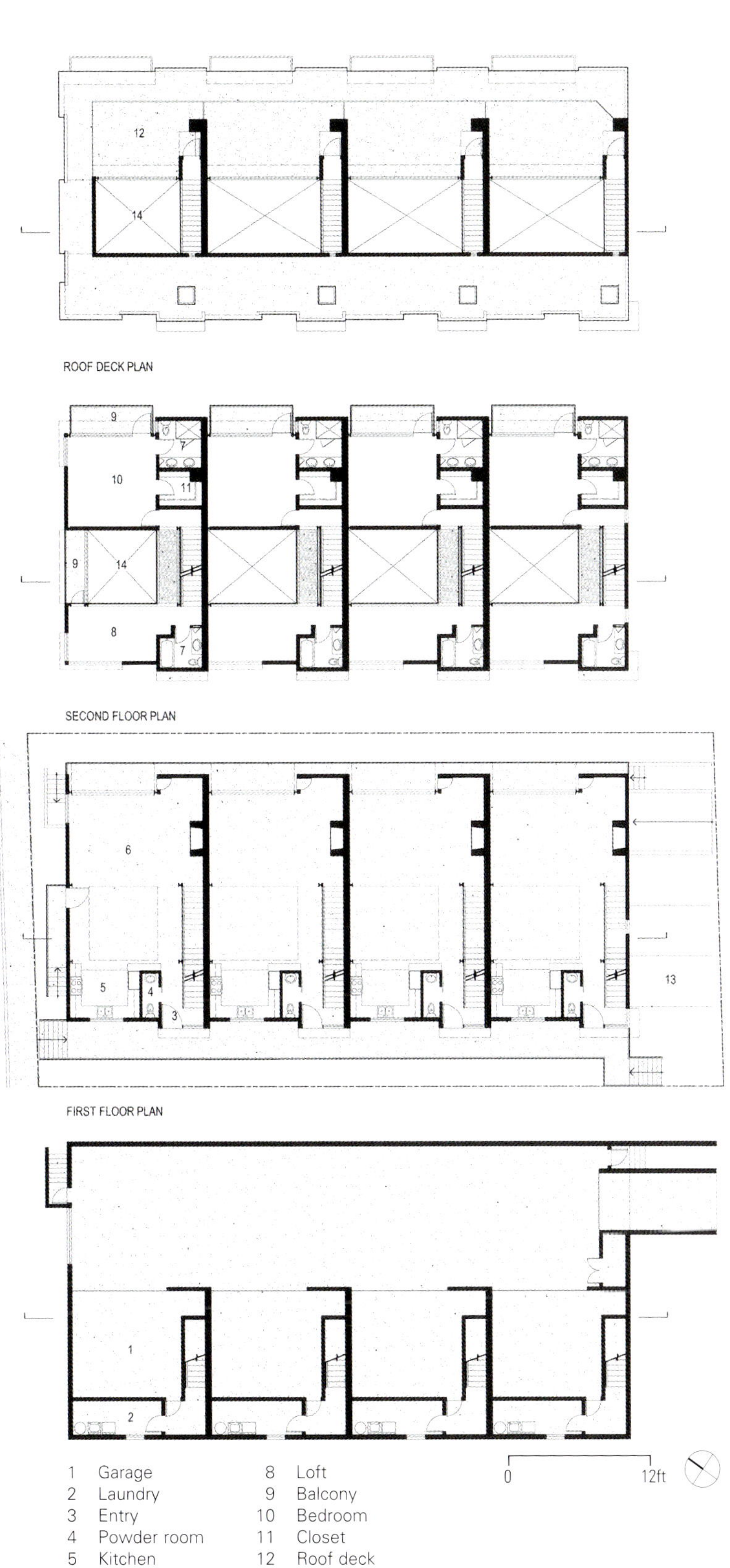

1 Garage
2 Laundry
3 Entry
4 Powder room
5 Kitchen
6 Living space
7 Bathroom
8 Loft
9 Balcony
10 Bedroom
11 Closet
12 Roof deck
13 Guest parking
14 Open to below

opposite Glass roll-up door opens space to outside
Photography Elon Shoenholtz
top Plans from ground floor to roof deck
top right View of glass roll-up door opened
right Open stairs allow views throughout
Photography Lawrence Manning

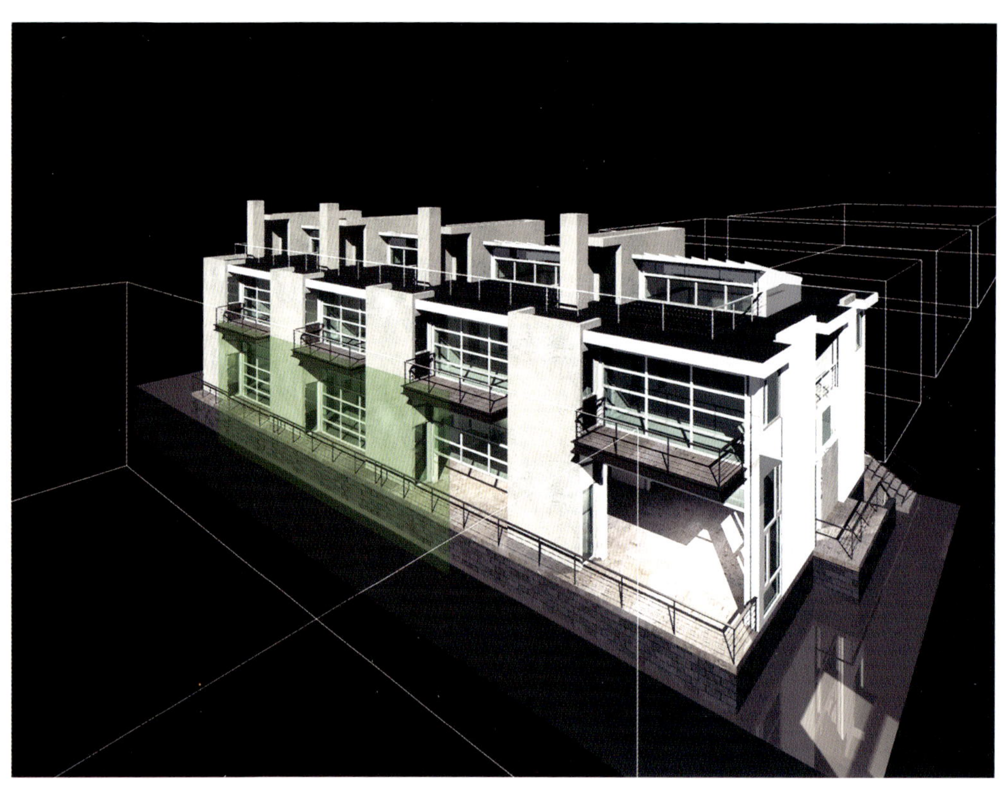

top	Units have generous windows toward beach views
bottom	Each unit enjoys roof deck views
opposite	Exposed steel structure and stairs contrast with walls
Photography	Elon Shoenholtz

Rollins Square

Boston, Massachusetts, USA

CBT Architects

below Overview of Rollins Square development
bottom Site plan
opposite Six-story apartment building with street-level retail

Stemming from its commitment to provide residential opportunities for families of all incomes, the Archdiocese of Boston developed Rollins Square as a model for a modern, mixed-income community that combines market-rate, moderately priced, low-income housing in a high-quality condominium complex. Rollins Square unites the Victorian architectural traditions of Boston's South End landmarks district with the industrial character of nearby warehouses that converge at the site.

The complex is arranged as a series of connected clusters that respond directly to the surrounding streetscape. Along with 184 residential units, the 376,000-square-foot project includes ground-level retail and a 200-space parking facility in an area where parking is scarce.

Designed as a grouping of six-story buildings and four-story townhouses, Rollins Square fosters a sense of community while allowing for a range of diverse domestic environments that vary in size from one-bedroom apartments to three-bedroom duplexes. Apartments are located in four corner buildings clad in multi-colored brick, which surround the new townhouses at the middle of the complex. The buildings' scale, massing, and materials are directly informed by three existing row-houses that were located on the site and integrated with the new construction. Because the project is broken down into a series of smaller parts, Rollins Square harmonizes with the existing cityscape but does not overwhelm it.

The project's form and organization are derived from the South End's traditional organization of buildings along public squares. At the center of the project, the buildings wrap around a central courtyard that gives the residents a shared sense of place. The open spaces of the South End are also reflected in ground-level patios, French balconies that offer views of the South End's existing green spaces, and rooftop decks.

The complex also maintains the pedestrian orientation of the South End neighborhood which remains one of this area's best assets. Retail spaces line the busy Washington Street corridor, and numerous private entrances activate the major streets, including townhouse stoops. Brick sidewalks, American elm trees, traditional cast-iron street lights, and seating walls serve as social gathering places for residents and members of the larger community.

ONE WAY

opposite Development combines six- and four-story buildings
bottom left Four-story townhouses occupy center
bottom right Courtyards are sprinkled throughout site
bottom Bricks with stone accents mediate scale

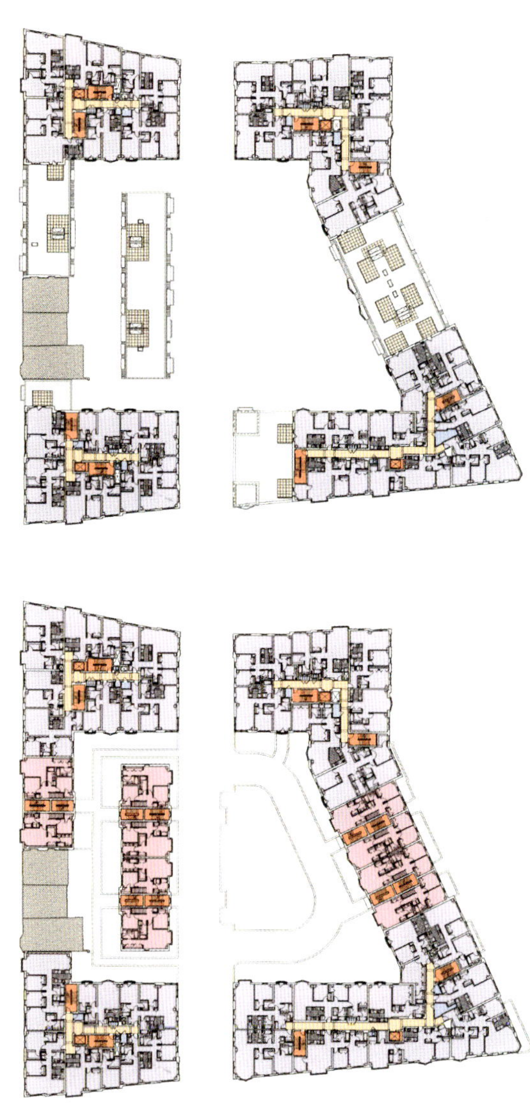

top Ground-level and upper-floor plans
opposite Central open space encourages community

bottom	Overview of central open space
opposite top left	Unit interiors have generous windows
opposite top right	Corner unit with overview of city
opposite below	Pedestrian scale is found throughout
Photography	Robert Benson Photography and Mark Flannery

K Lofts

San Diego, California, USA

Jonathan Segal, Architect

The K Lofts project is adaptive reuse, affordable and sustainable rental housing. The project was designed with a participatory design process creating positive connections between and among residents, community stakeholders, local government officials, and civic groups. The architect/developer worked closely with the community for nine months to ensure a project that is well received by the neighborhood and provides much needed affordable housing in San Diego.

The result of this process is a combination of public and private spaces that enhance human scale and further promote social interaction and shared use of space, while helping to revitalize this deteriorating community, and enhancing the community's physical fabric. The project was built at a cost of $82 per square foot and utilized no governmental subsidy.

K Lofts is a collection of simple yet bold architectural forms composed to create a nine-unit loft building on a 9000-square-foot urban property in the Golden Hill area of downtown San Diego. The former Circle K convenience store and gas station was saved and integrated into the new design to minimize the amount of demolition and adapt the existing building to a new use.

The new building integrates urban living environments with a mixture of very low-income (50 percent of median income) affordable and market-rate rental units with each unit containing large private outdoor spaces and generous glazing. The sustainable project provides 50 percent renewable electricity and a unit set-aside for low-income families.

left Affordable steel mesh accents exterior
opposite Floating volumes lend a sense of lightness

top	Simple detailing distinguishes interiors
right	Vertical elements contain dramatic spaces
opposite top	Complex is a recycled convenience store
opposite middle	Elevations transform existing buildings
opposite bottom	Open space inserted between wings

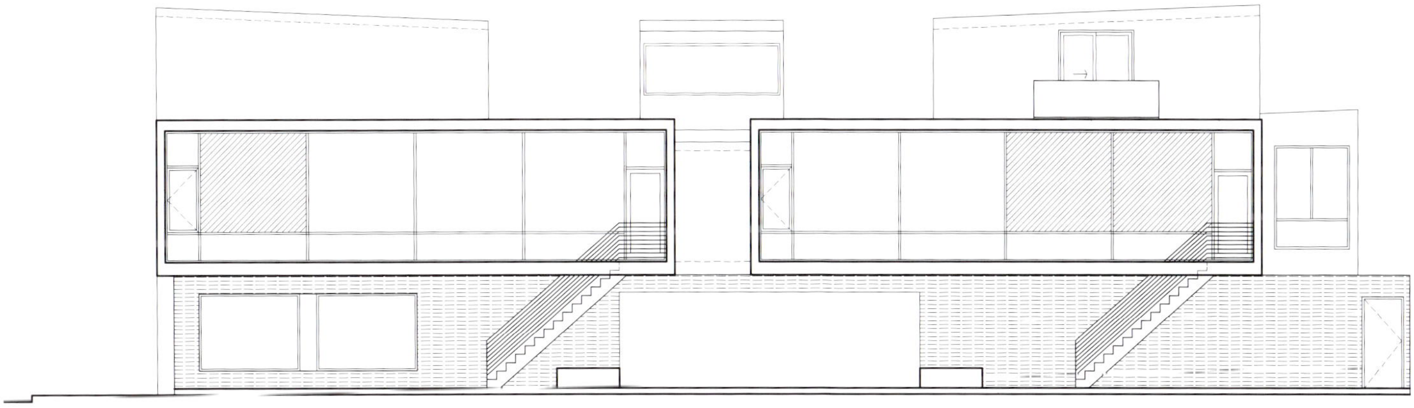

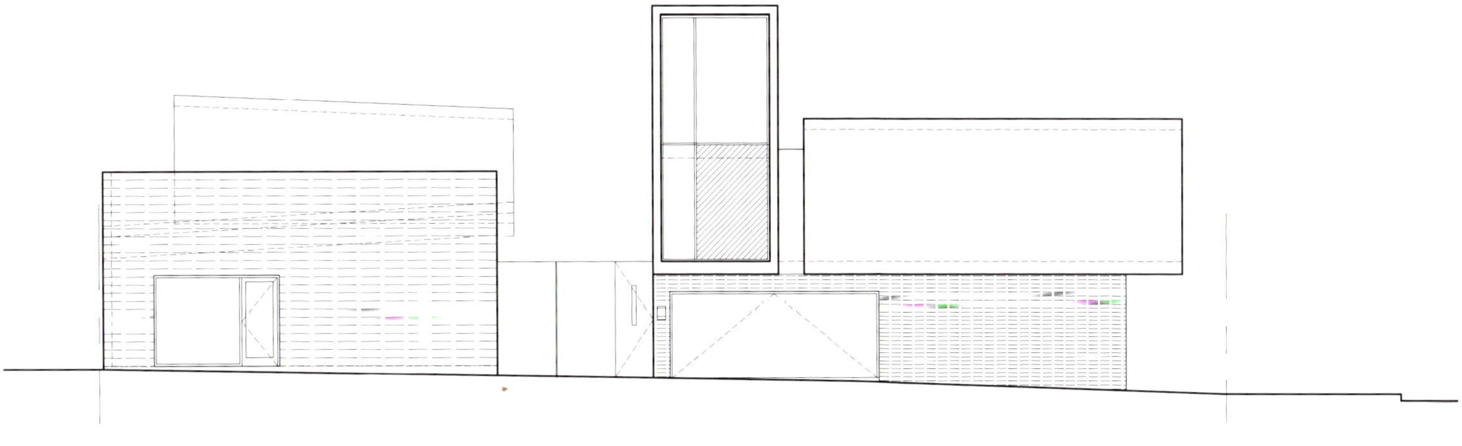

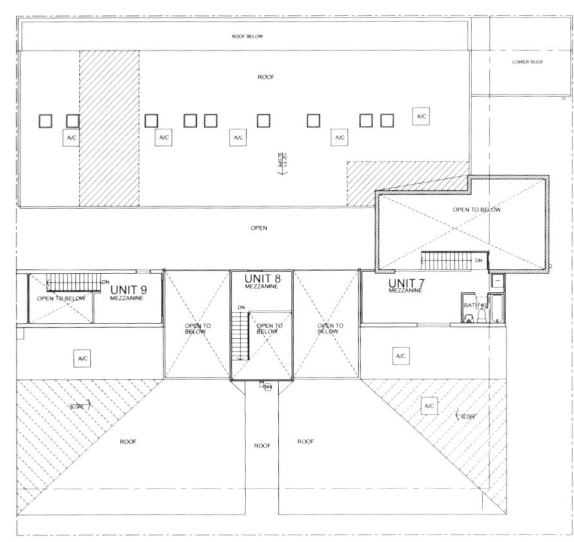
ROOF
OPEN
OPEN TO BELOW
UNIT 9
MEZZANINE
UNIT 8
MEZZANINE
UNIT 7
MEZZANINE
ROOF
ROOF
ROOF

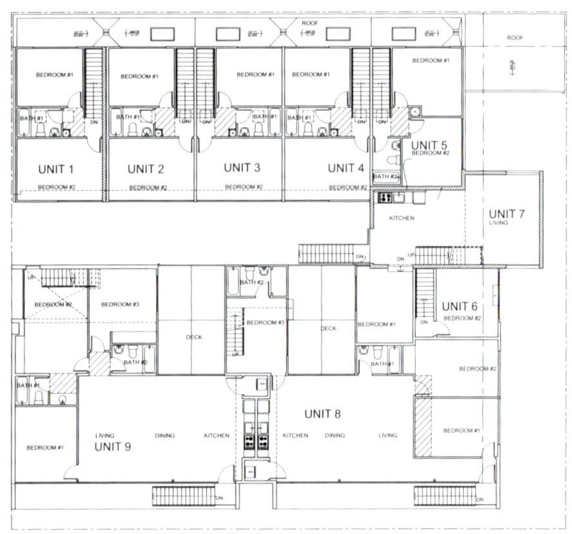
ROOF
UNIT 1
UNIT 2
UNIT 3
UNIT 4
UNIT 5
UNIT 7
LIVING
KITCHEN
UNIT 6
DECK
DECK
UNIT 8
UNIT 9
LIVING
DINING
KITCHEN

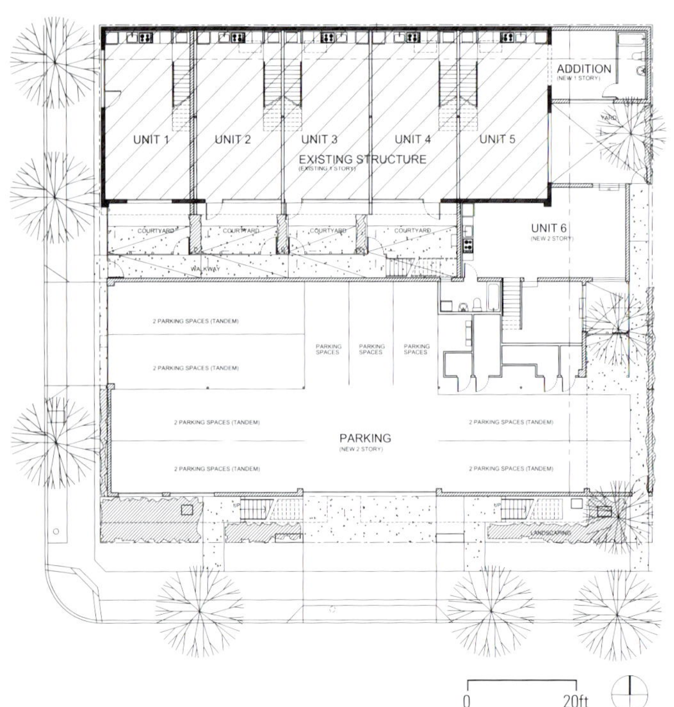
ADDITION
(NEW 1 STORY)
UNIT 1
UNIT 2
UNIT 3
UNIT 4
UNIT 5
EXISTING STRUCTURE
UNIT 6
(NEW 2 STORY)
PARKING
(NEW 2 STORY)
0
20ft

far left, top to bottom Top-, middle-, and ground-level plans
top left Steel stairs are affordable yet elegant
bottom left Open riser stair allows interior views
top Courtyard access from street
right Interior of courtyard oasis
Photography Paul Body

Commerce Street
Townhomes

Dallas, Texas, USA

Ron Wommack Architect

This new eight-unit townhome project is located east of downtown Dallas, in an historic industrial neighborhood that is now finding new life in residential development. The design of the Commerce Street units attempts to capture the messy vitality of the transitioning area through variegated forms, a variety of materials, and a mix of large and small volumes. The units are 27 feet wide and average 2700 square feet in area.

The units are organized in section rather than by plan, as is typically the case. This sectional quality allows for great efficiency of garages with bedroom spaces above. This also permits for a freer interpretation of the public spaces. Generous spaces nearly three stories high penetrate the units, opening a well of light and volume that becomes an architectural celebration.

The use of concrete block, corrugated sheets of galvanized metal, copper shingles, and galvanized chain-link fence posts create an alchemy of unique dwelling spaces. Roof forms are used to dramatic effect, giving the units a heroic quality. The interiors express the materials employed, which are rendered under the natural light that each unit captures. The difference in volumes allows for the use of passive solar strategies such as clerestory natural lighting. Other passive solar qualities include a shaded roof deck.

The scale and materiality created by this new townhome project connects the area's industrial past with today's lifestyle, with its use of low maintenance materials that will age gracefully, acknowledging the passage of time.

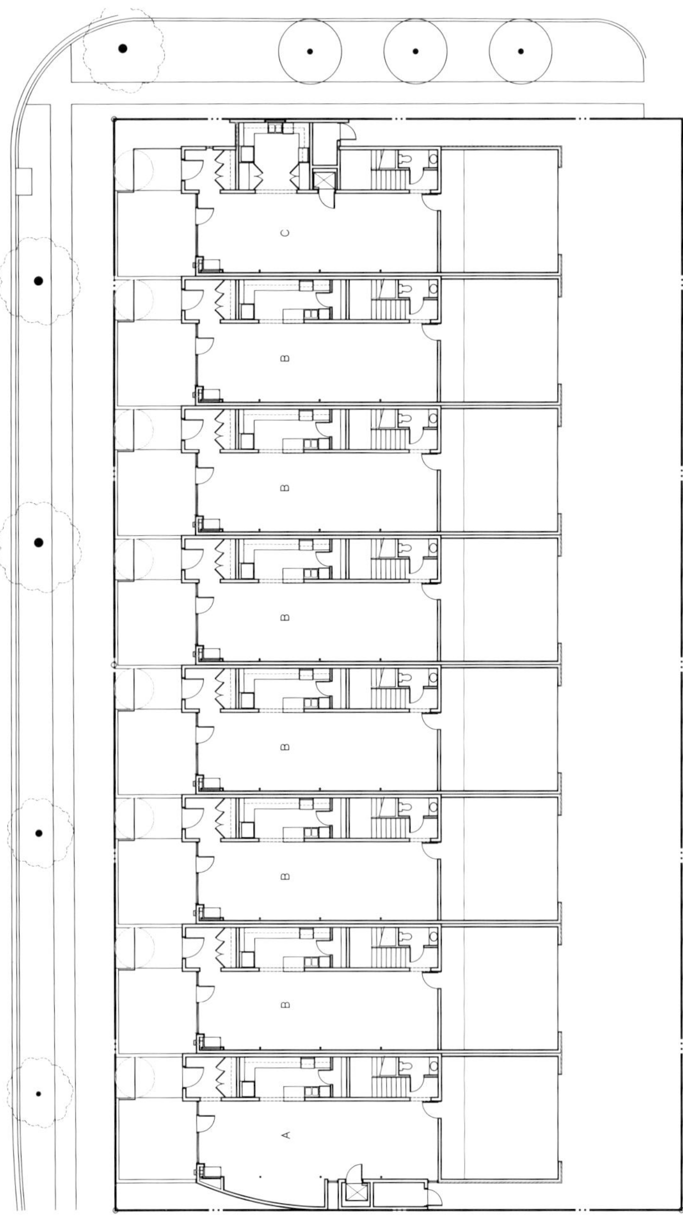

left Ground-level plan of complex
opposite Dramatic roof surmounts each unit

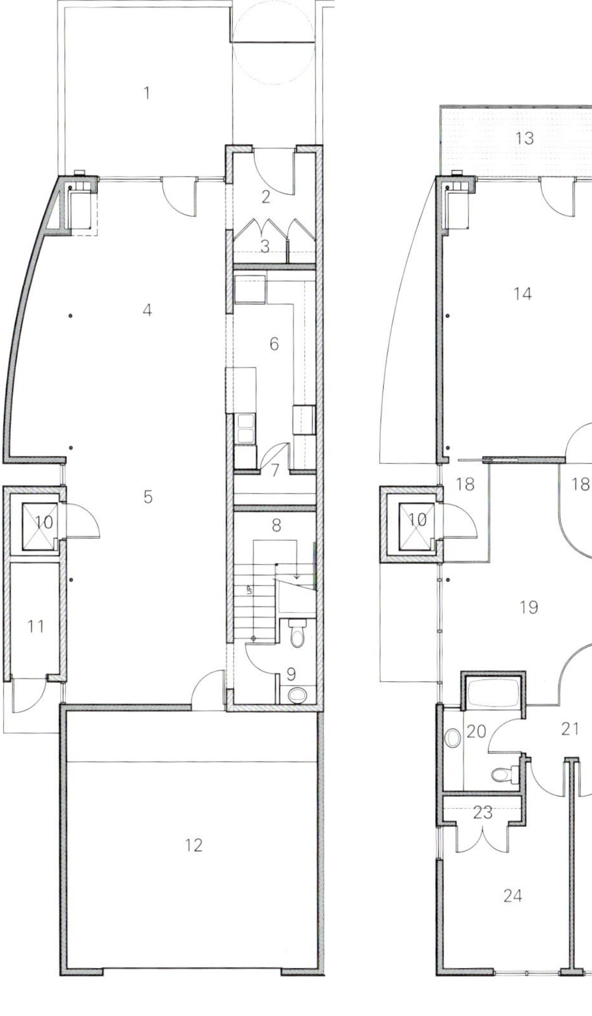

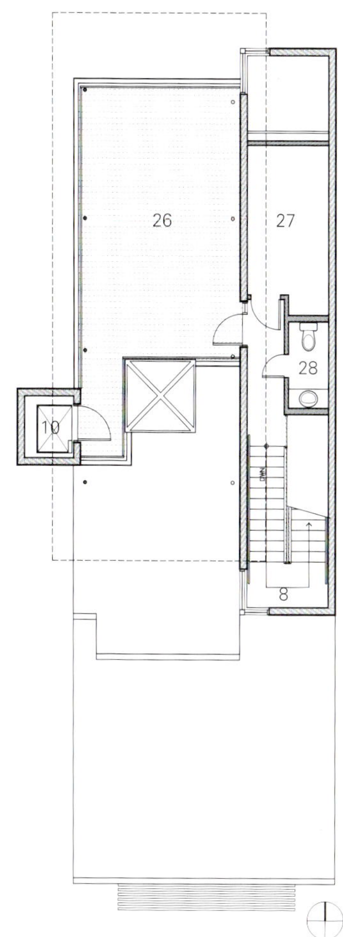

1 Entry court
2 Entry
3 Coats
4 Living
5 Dining
6 Kitchen
7 Pantry
8 Stair
9 Powder room 1
10 Elevator
11 Equipment
12 Garage
13 Porch
14 Master bedroom
15 Master bathroom
16 Toilet/shower
17 Master closet
18 Balcony
19 Atrium
20 Bathroom
21 Laundry
22 Closet
23 Bedroom 2
24 Bedroom 3
25 Roof deck
26 Mech
27 Powder room 2

opposite top The units have a rhythm along the street
opposite bottom Side view hints at sectional character
top Individual unit plan
left Units as they address the street
above Complex from the back

top left Each unit contains private outdoor space
top middle Living areas are open and spacious
top right Surprising expanses of space within
bottom Kitchen opens to entertainment space
opposite Staircase weaves through spatial envelope
Photography Charles Davis Smith

11th Avenue
Townhomes

Escondido, California, USA

Studio E Architects

bottom Site plan of units facing onto circulation spine
opposite Units are individually identified by color and pop-outs

Escondido lies 45 miles north of San Diego in a broad valley surrounded by rocky hills. The area was identified in the 1920s as an ideal climate for avocados and citrus and began its slow growth based around those crops. The 11th Avenue Townhomes are built in a down-on-its-heels neighborhood of modest pre-war bungalows which originally housed the families of pickers, packers, and tradespeople. This older downtown neighborhood is within a redevelopment district and has been the site of two other affordable housing projects by the architects.

This project provides rental units at below-market rates for working families. The unit mix includes two-, three-, and four-bedroom plans. There are 14 two-story townhomes and two flats with one unit reserved for a disabled occupant. Common facilities include a meeting hall, laundry, tot lot, and a shared vegetable garden.

Two vertebral rows of attached townhomes front onto a narrow tree-lined lane. This communal axis serves as both automobile and pedestrian circulation. Midway along its length, the lane breaks open into a protected plaza/courtyard. This space is developed as the place of both formal and informal gathering. A barn-like meeting hall looks across a shady plaza to an open lawn that includes a colorful children's play structure. The common laundry facility is located at this quadrangle as is the office of the resident manager. Overflow parking and the shared vegetable garden anchor the south end of the lane.

The units are designed with simple, easy-to-furnish plans with a minimum of interior circulation. Small rear patio/gardens provide valuable private outdoor space. Construction is wood framing on concrete slab foundations. Exteriors are finished in stucco and cement fiberboard horizontal siding.

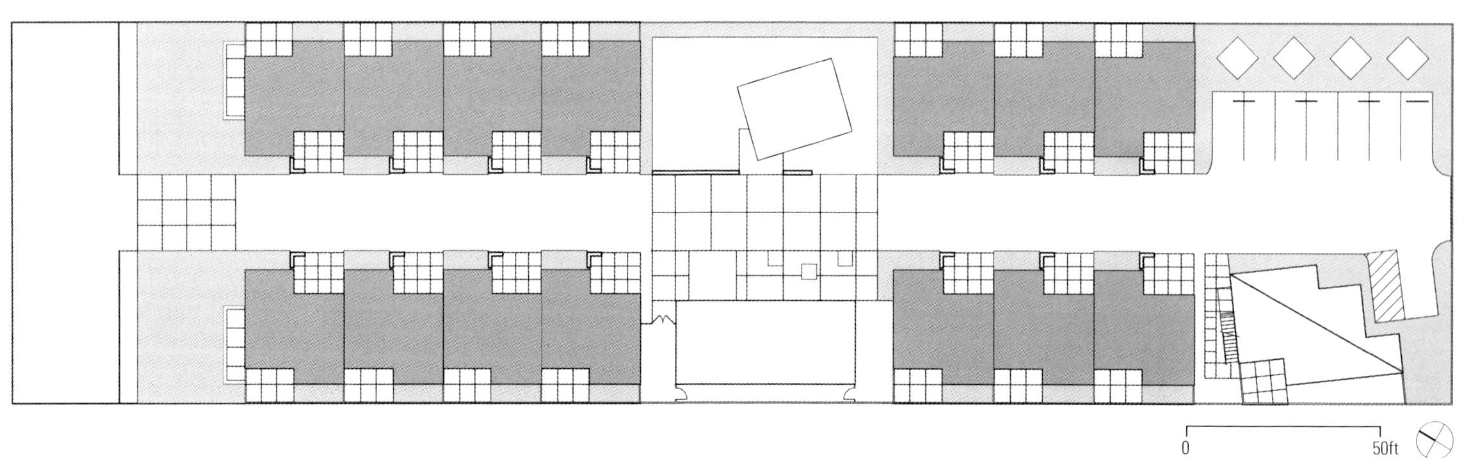

top Circulation spine through the development's center
opposite top Common area is a place for community gathering
opposite bottom Complex as it fronts onto the road

opposite top Community space with its exposed roof truss
opposite bottom Interiors have simple, affordable finishes
bottom Green courtyard is found at the center
Photography Jim Brady/Brady Architectural Photography

Box & One
Lofts

Portland, Oregon, USA

Fletcher Farr Ayotte and Kevin Cavenaugh

bottom Development's Box (at left) and One (at right)
opposite A single apartment is found above a bistro

This 7318-square-foot project (for which intern architect Kevin Cavenaugh of Fletcher Farr Ayotte served as developer and designer) comprises two separate buildings on a city infill lot on the east side of the river: a large building (Box), which includes four lofts atop a bakery, and the smaller building (& One), which has one live/work unit above a wine bistro.

To blur the line between indoor and outdoor spaces, aside from four small aluminum casement egress windows and a small storefront for the bakery, virtually every window is a glass sectional garage door customized to meet energy codes. At least 85 square feet of window space in each unit can be completely opened, transforming interior spaces such as living rooms into porches. Radiant concrete floors are used to heat the five residential units, which allows for the garage door windows to be open more often in the temperate Portland climate.

Exposed concrete block, concrete floors, tongue-and-groove car-decking at the mezzanines, and exposed roof trusses, steel beams, and pan decking allow for an economical building that was constructed for $107 per square foot.

Three percent of the construction budget was spent on public art. Lee Kelly, a metal sculptor, designed and installed a two-ton stainless steel piece on the prominent prow of the Box. This corner is angled at 75 degrees to address a major intersection one block to the north. The piece is backlit to allow for the positive image to shine by day while the negative image glows by night.

top to bottom Top, middle, and ground-floor plans
opposite Box wing with glowing public sculpture
opposite left Bistro interior spills onto street
opposite right Apartment sports glass roll-up door wall
Photography Gene Faulkner, Genefaulkner.com
Brian Foulkes

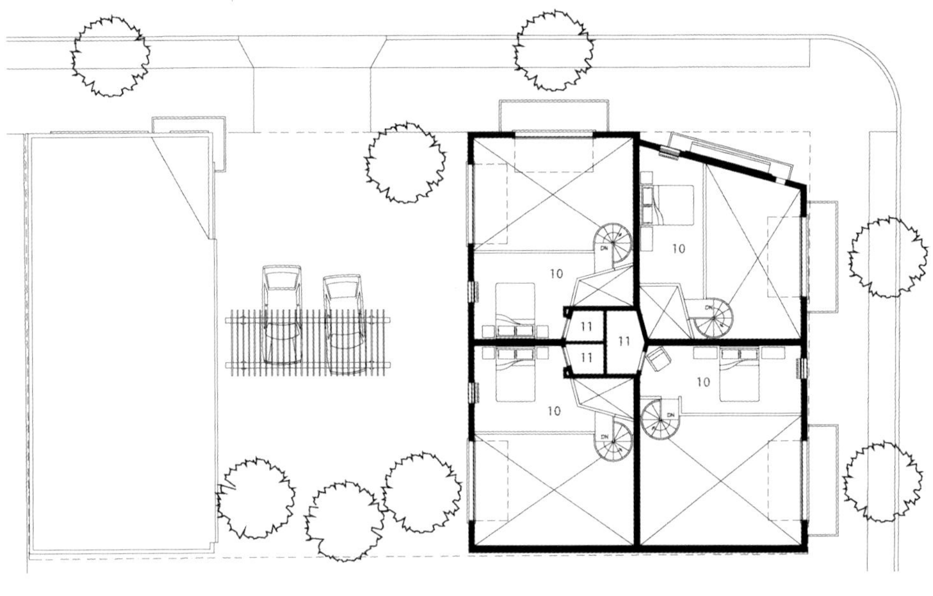

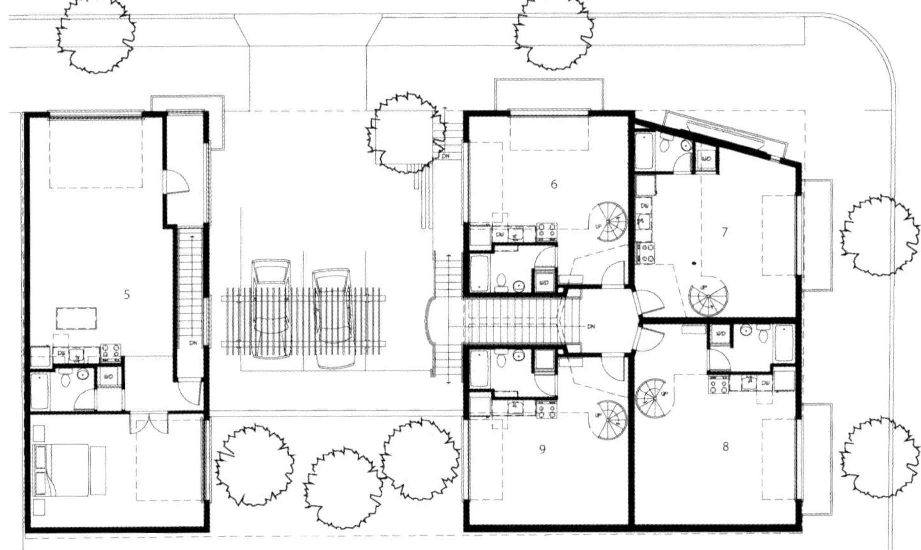

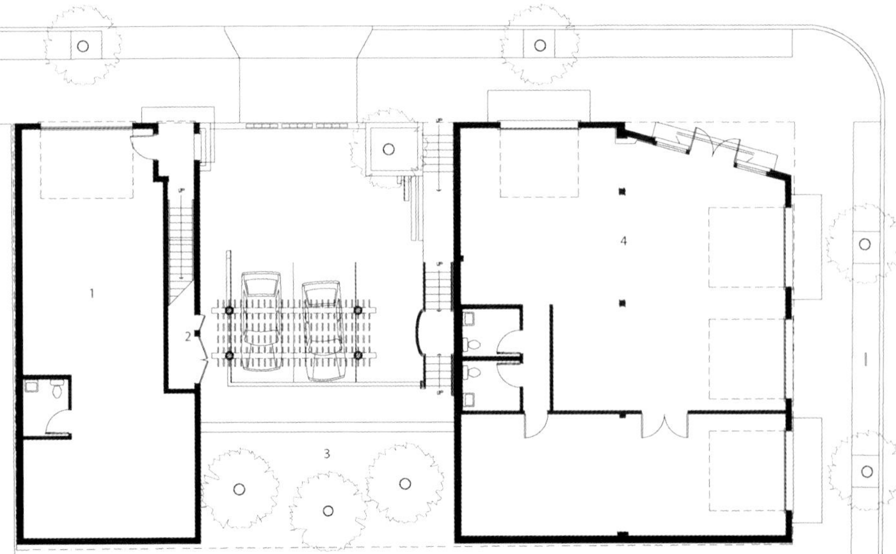

1 Noble Rot Wine Bar
2 Trash/recycle
3 Noble Rot Garden
4 Crema Bakery and Café
5 Noble Rot live/work
6 Loft A
7 Loft B
8 Loft C
9 Loft D
10 Lofted space
11 Closet

8th and Howard
Apartments

San Francisco, California, USA

David Baker + Partners

This five-story building in San Francisco's South of Market area combines 74 one-, two-, or three-bedroom family apartments with 88 studios and six community rooms, a parking garage, and lobby spaces for the four floors of housing above. This affordable housing development makes room for an eclectic mix of artists, immigrants, veterans, families, and twenty-somethings—a true microcosm of the city, with a density of 155 units per acre.

Reduced parking frees space for a childcare center and 19,000 square feet of commercial space serving the neighborhood, including a market. A car-share pod is located in the garage providing an alternative to owning a car. Major bus lines, rapid transportation, and bike lanes border the property for a wealth of transportation. Natoma Alley provides a drop-off and pick-up point for the childcare center, marked by its distinctive curved walls.

Semi-public courtyards not only provide outdoor areas for resident functions but also break up the urban edge and offer unexpected views to neighbors and nearby pedestrians. The gap in the urban edge provides a view into the softer interior open space, sharing it with the civic whole. Entrances to the housing are through semi-public landscaped courtyards that also serve as outdoor green space for public functions and also as a safe play space for children. Custom-designed steel gates give the garden spaces a sense of enclosure. The architect collaborated with a local artist, South Park Fabricators, on the design of the custom steel gate and fountain at the main entrance. The bold blues and yellows and the addition of a geometric mural along the 8th Street elevation further enliven the building.

bottom Curved wall of childcare center
opposite Private courtyard offers semi-public space

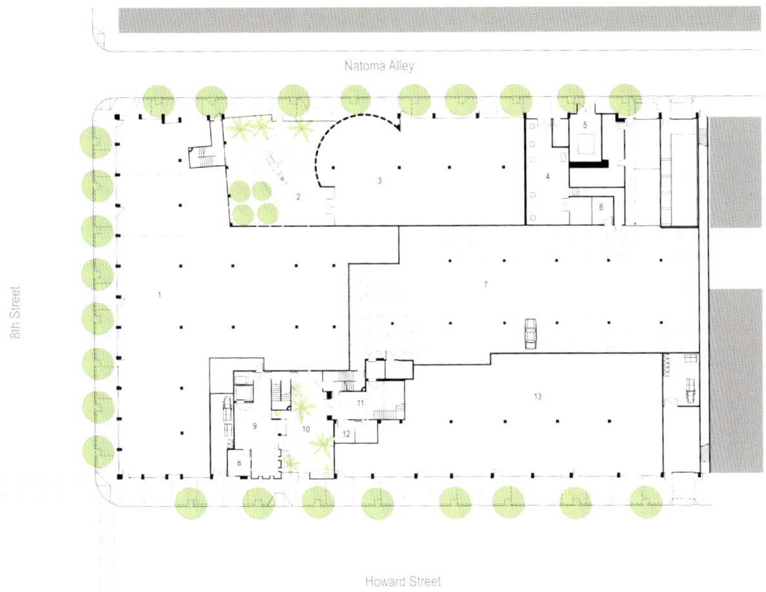

Natoma Alley

8th Street

Howard Street

1 Commercial (grocery)
2 Childcare courtyard & play area
3 Childcare
4 Boiler
5 Transformer
6 Storage
7 Parking garage
8 Office
9 Studio lobby
10 Entry court
11 Apartment lobby
12 Office
13 Commercial

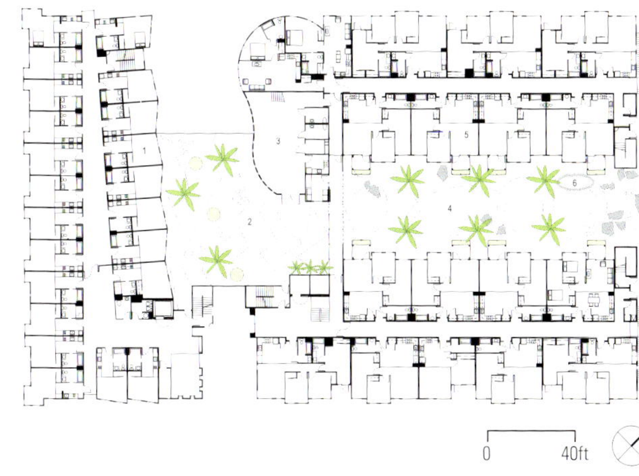

0 40ft

1 Studio units
2 Courtyard
3 Program space
4 Courtyard
5 Apartment units
6 Sandbox

opposite top Façade is a play of white and black materials
opposite bottom Elevation along 8th Street uses bold colors
top left Lower-level plan with car-share pod
top right Ground-level plan
left Custom-designed steel gates to garden
Photography Michelle Peckham

Rose/Knox
Townhouses

Houston, Texas, USA

Donna Kacmar, Christopher Craig, Mary Ann Young

bottom Exterior materials express living and utility spaces
opposite left Affordable materials are left in natural state
opposite right Each unit has its own private staircase

Three former architecture school classmates who are now professional architects joined forces to enter first-time homeownership by designing and building three townhouses for themselves. The investigation focused on how three individual units might be developed within an inner-city neighborhood using an efficient configuration of 1600 square feet of living space per townhouse. Low-cost and low-maintenance materials prevalent in the warehouses and bungalows of the diverse neighborhood were explored.

The design provides each townhouse unit with its own profile and identifiable front door, expressed with a contemporary architectural language. Each unit is composed of a large rectangular "living" box joined by a recessed, interstitial "utility" box. Within each unit, the ground floor is devoted to a small entry foyer with access to a one-car garage, mechanical space, and a private staircase. On the second floor, the utility box contains a small kitchen (each one laid out a bit differently) and a hallway leading to a completely open living and dining area. The end units have small balconies off the dining area. A small half-bath is tucked into the landing of the second floor stair. The third floor of each unit is slightly different, containing a bathroom in the utility wing, and a bedroom with a large studio space, or two bedrooms in the living box.

The exterior of the townhouses incorporates a Galvalume clad "living" box and a cementitious fiberboard clad "utility" box sitting on a load-bearing concrete masonry unit first floor. Prefabricated floor trusses, concrete masonry firewalls and plywood decking were left exposed to maintain a construction cost of $50 per square foot.

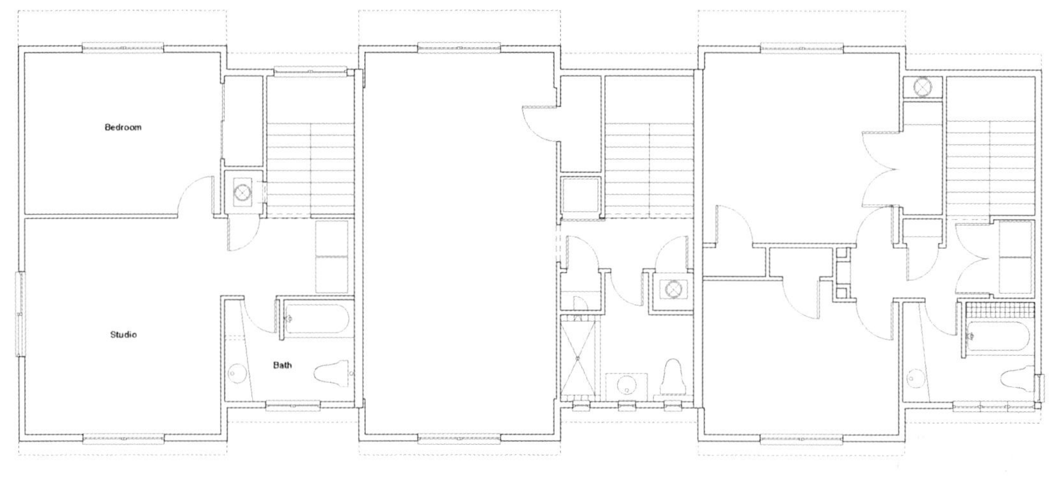
Bedroom
Studio
Bath

Living
Dining
Kitchen
Living
Dining
Kitchen
Living
Dining
Kitchen

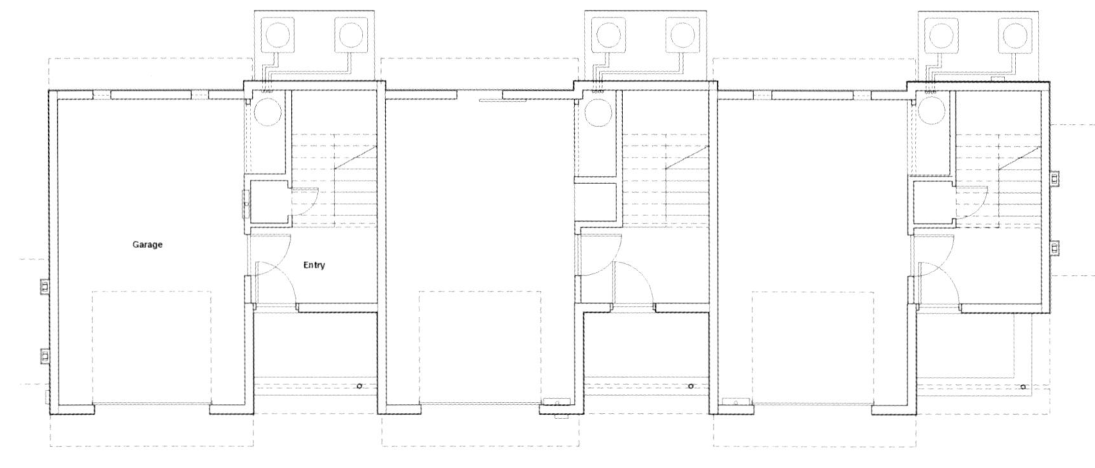
Garage
Entry

opposite top	Third-floor plan
opposite middle	Second-floor plan
opposite bottom	Ground-floor plan
left	Exposed floor trusses in living area
bottom	Living units surmount garage level
Photography	Courtesy of the architects

Loyola Village

San Francisco, California, USA

Seidel Holzman

bottom Site plan of the steeply sloped complex
opposite Loyola Village as it meets the street

Loyola Village provides 136 apartments at the University of San Francisco for students, staff, and faculty. Situated on a steep slope at the northern edge of campus, the project is designed to define Anza Street with a scale appropriate to the adjacent residential neighborhood. Individual stoop entries, bay-windows, color, and roofline variations enliven the streetscape.

Although technically a four-story building, the project actually has six levels as it terraces down the slope. The stepped section permits numerous units to take advantage of city views to the north, all the way to the Golden Gate Bridge and the Marin Headlands.

A terraced pedestrian mews leads up from Anza Street through Loyola Village to the main part of campus, creating a new urban connection from the neighborhood to the north into the heart of the campus. The parking garage is bermed into the slope, with townhouses placed on top of and in front of it in order to screen it from public view. Landscaped courtyards are located above the garage and are overlooked by apartments as well as townhouses.

A material palette of stucco and terracotta clay roof tiles helps to tie the project into the prevailing character of the campus architecture. However, the project maintains a contemporary air through the use of large areas of glazing and a modern sensibility in detailing.

By providing a wide variety of residential accommodations, from studios to three-bedroom townhouses, the project appeals to a diverse spectrum of the university population and has strengthened the sense of community on campus.

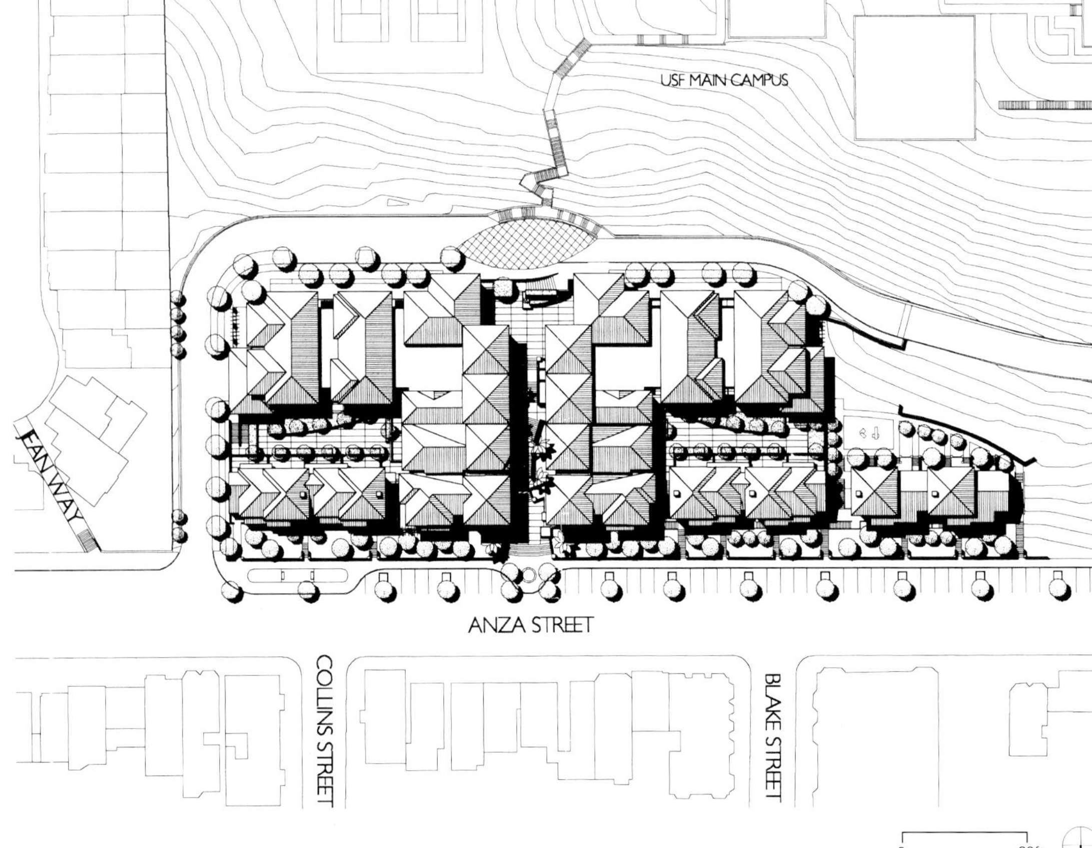

DRIVEWAY
0
30ft

331
UNIVERSITY of SAN FRANCISCO
USF
Scholarship and Service
Since 1855

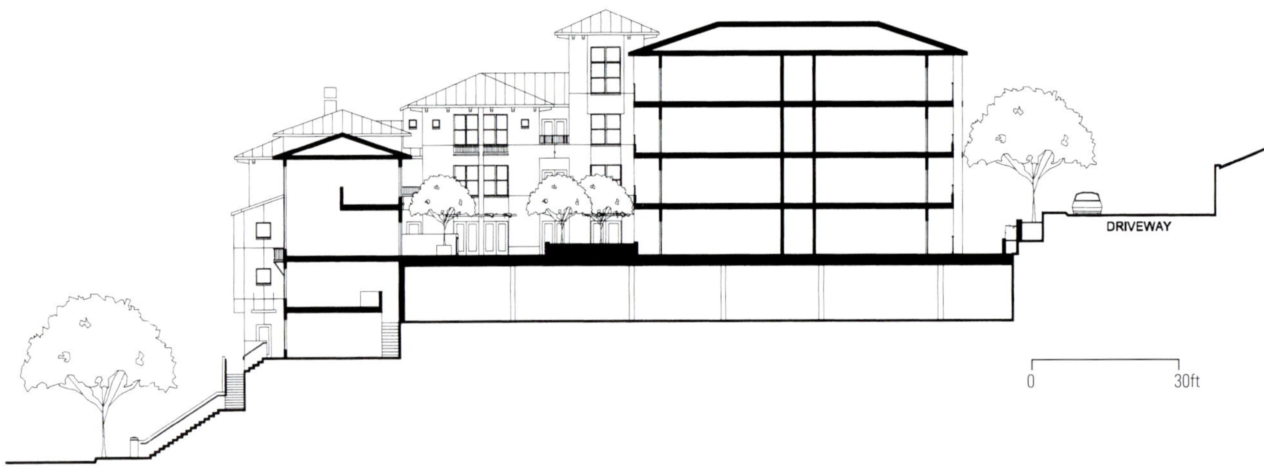

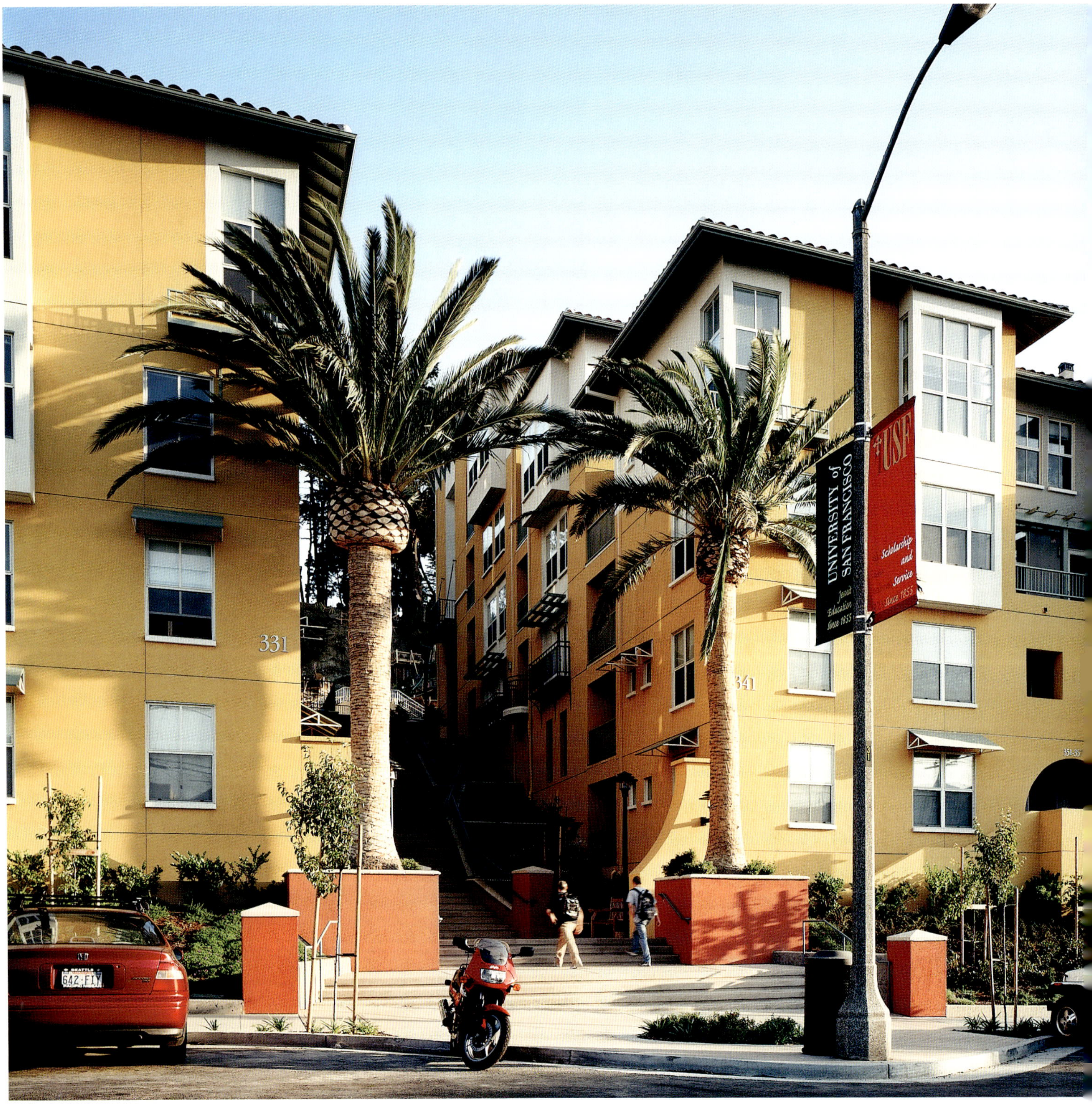

top left Section shows how building negotiates slope
opposite Anza Street elevation, as building climbs
top View from above shows complex descending

top Large windows permit generous views
right One-bedroom unit plans
opposite top Double-height living area maximizes light
opposite bottom Unit plans look outward toward views

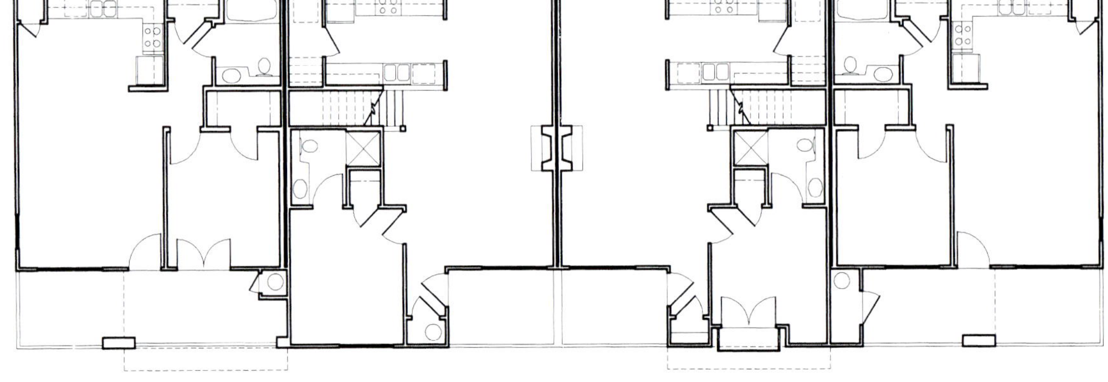

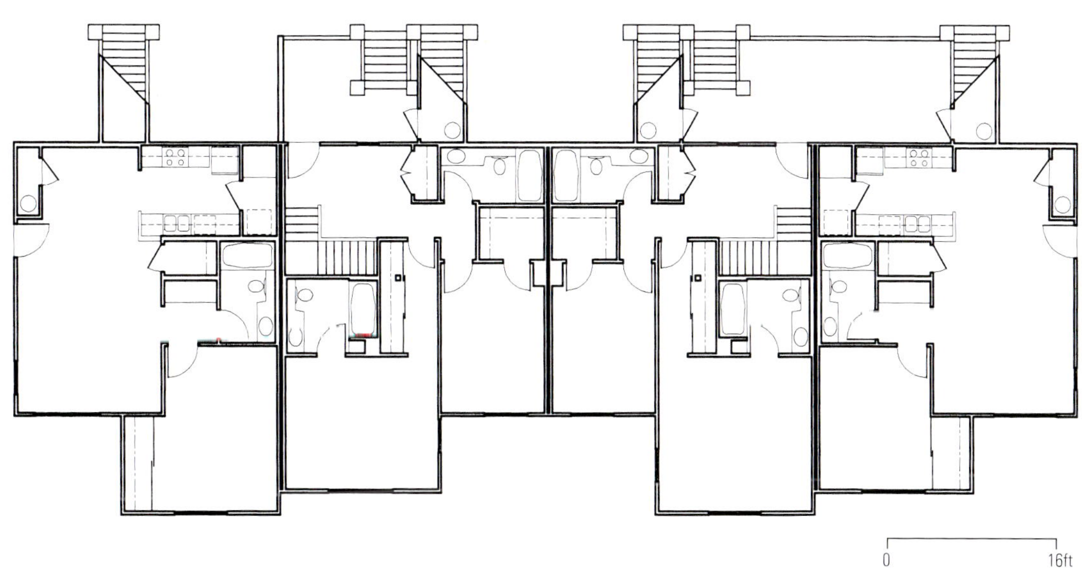
0
16ft

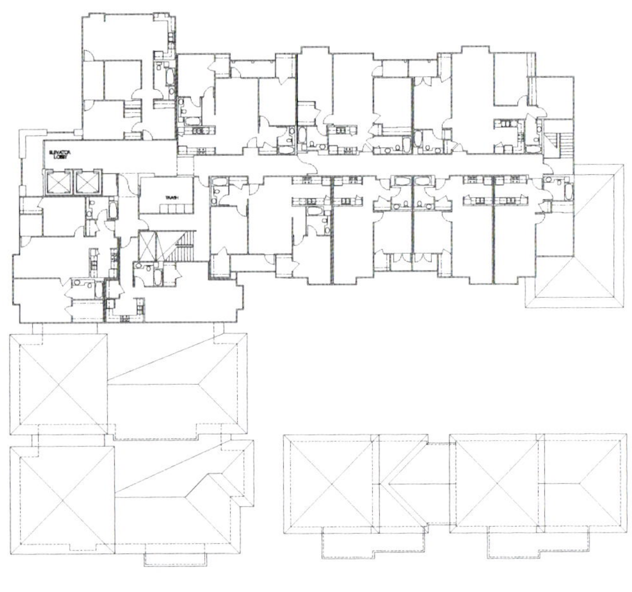

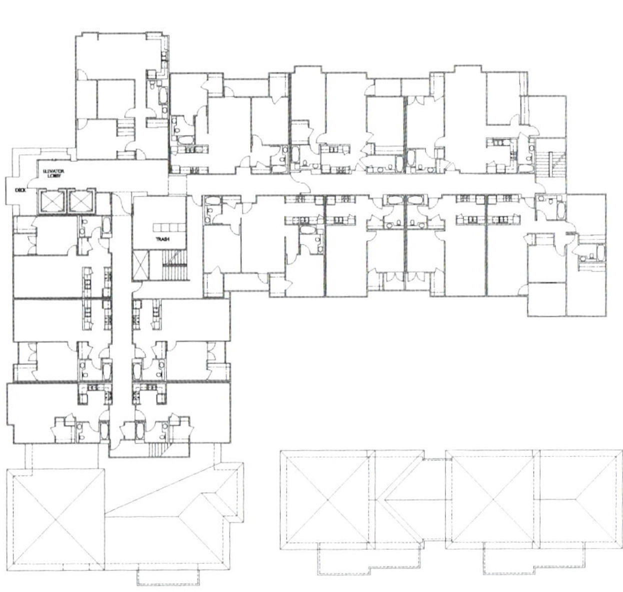

0
30ft

opposite, top to bottom Top, middle, and lower level plans
top View from promontory toward Anza Street and city
Photography Russell Abraham

Blake Street
Flats

Denver, Colorado, USA

Humphries Poli Architects

bottom Blake Street elevation with anchor at corner
opposite Colorful metal panels distinguish façade

Blake Street Flats is a three-story, 24-unit building located in one of Denver's historic districts, a short walk from the central business district. An infill project amongst historic homes and industrial warehouses, it introduces affordable housing appropriate to its setting. Blake Street is part of a larger development, Curtis Park Redevelopment, involving a partnership of private developers, the Denver Housing Authority, and the City and County of Denver.

The area's extant housing mix is wide ranging: single-story duplexes, recently renovated Victorian-era mansions, flat-roofed row houses, and two-story brick "Denver Squares." A historic warehouse district filled with loft projects forms the district's western border.

The design process involved a diverse group of community stakeholders and former residents of the area's previously failed public housing projects. Bi-monthly meetings were conducted with a Design Advisory Committee. Working within the neighborhood's process and being responsive to suggestions resulted in a multifamily residence that helps revitalize the neighborhood by enhancing its physical fabric while increasing the opportunities for social interaction.

The architectural solution adopts the neighborhood's palette of exposed concrete frames, corrugated steel, and humble historic images and combines them into unique, modern units sensitive to the area's historic context. Brightly colored corrugated metal boxes float above a continuous first-floor porch with expansive windows in each unit that open onto the street and let in the abundant Colorado daylight. The "L" shaped plan holds the street edges, while defining a courtyard at the building's rear for service access and parking.

top Units echo the townhouse forms of older houses
opposite top Location of project in Curtis Park Redevelopment
opposite Entry to second story units
Photography Ed LaCasse

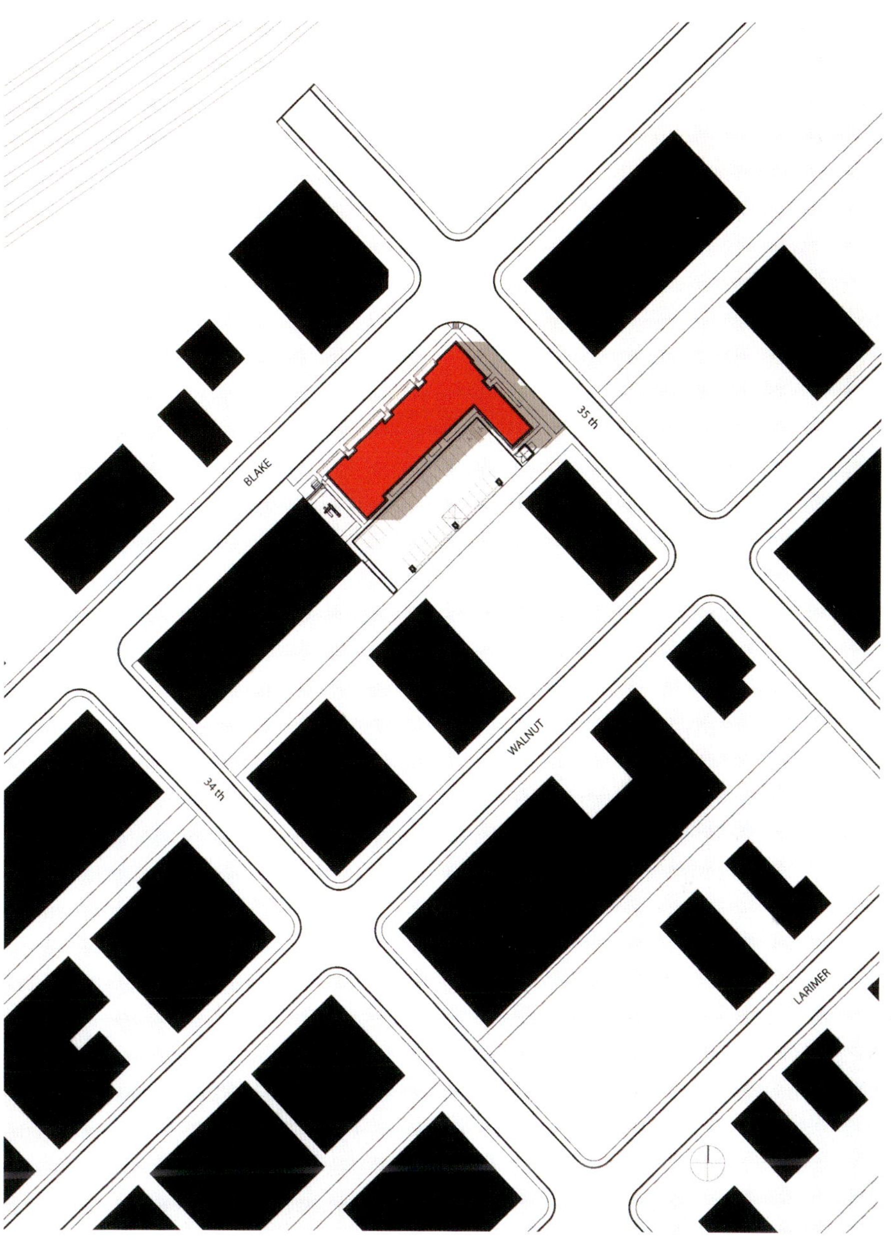
BLAKE
35 th
WALNUT
34 th
LARIMER

HomeSafe

San Jose, California, USA

Studio E Architects

bottom Site plan is organized around green open space
opposite Community building anchors end of courtyard
opposite bottom Colorful façades face open green space

This project's design challenge was to create a secure and emotionally uplifting environment for women and their families fleeing abuse.

HomeSafe is a unique collaboration of seven non-profit domestic violence and social service agencies formed to create transitional housing as an important stepping-stone between shelters and permanent residences. The co-housing model—in which four families share a townhouse—grants a combination of private and shared space offering the women both the privacy and community they need to regain control of their lives.

The site plan and the 25 units are designed around this concept of private and shared on a site slightly larger than one acre. Three separate residential buildings front onto green open space. Each building contains two townhouses, each with four units. The units share living, dining, kitchen, and laundry facilities in each of the townhouses.

From courtyard to porch, kitchen to lounge, and bedroom suite to sleeping alcove, residents are offered an increasingly protected setting. Generous openings and careful siting fill the spaces with sunlight. High-sloping ceilings lend an unexpected expansiveness to the communal areas of the homes. A fourth building contains administrative offices and childcare facilities.

A light neutral-colored plaster was chosen for the sides of buildings facing property lines, while bright, warm hues enliven the courtyard faces of the homes. Saw-toothed metal roofs and deep awnings recall the Santa Clara Valley's agricultural past. The project entry is anchored by the daycare and community center building.

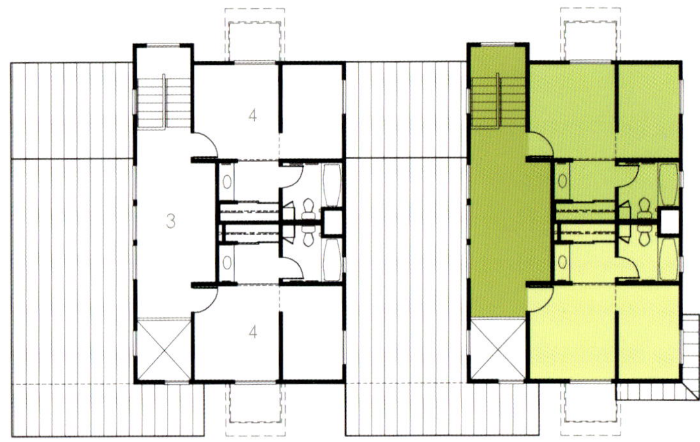

1 Kitchen
2 Dining Area
3 Living Room
4 Private suite
5 Laundry
6 Patio/Porch

opposite Townhouse ground-, and second-floor plans
opposite bottom Community building helps to define entry
top Trellises lends shade and scale
top right Kitchens and dining areas are shared by residents
bottom Courtyard lends a protected environment

top Sloped roofs reflect ceiling heights inside
top right Community gathers around green space
bottom Landscape design is simple and tranquil
opposite Low stone walls, concrete columns, and stucco exteriors
Photography Jeff Peters, Vantage Point Photography

Laconia
Lofts

Boston, Massachusetts, USA

Hacin + Associates

bottom Site plan showing living and working spaces
opposite top Laconia Lofts' entrance at the corner
opposite bottom Warehouse aesthetic relates to neighborhood

Laconia Lofts is the first new "ground-up construction" of affordable live/work artist spaces built in the eastern U.S. since the early 20th century. It is also the first significant new construction project completed in the burgeoning industrial area of Boston's South End. The project provides an important physical anchor at each of its major entry points: the Washington Street commercial district to the west and the Harrison Avenue arts district to the east.

Laconia Lofts is located at a key point of transition point between the South End Landmark District of brick Victorian townhouses and an arts district of warehouse lofts. The project is a bridge between these distinct areas, both architecturally and programmatically. Since construction, empty lots surrounding Laconia have been extensively rebuilt and Washington Street has undergone a major revitalization.

Comprised of 99 units of live/work condominiums (45 of them designated as affordable), commercial uses, and gallery space, the building incorporates the linear forms of its warehouse neighbors as well as the materials and rhythm of the townhouse district facing the Washington Street facade. The longer volume along Laconia Way meets the shorter Washington Street volume, where the two site-generated angles are resolved and marked by balconies and a central tower.

A contemporary interpretation of Victorian-era warehouses is expressed through massing, the use of two tones of brick, as well as by the introduction of metal elements that have an industrial aesthetic, including balconies and canopies that recall the district's heritage of decorative ironwork. Dark-gray windows run in horizontal groupings, parallel to the brick bands of color along Laconia Way. Larger expanses of glass at the front express the double-height penthouse spaces of the fifth floor.

Unit interiors are conceived as a bare-bone "canvas" in which owners can create their own designs, a corollary to the art being produced in the building. Simple and utilitarian fixtures serve artists' needs, and bare concrete floors and exposed mechanical systems lend an industrial atmosphere to the units.

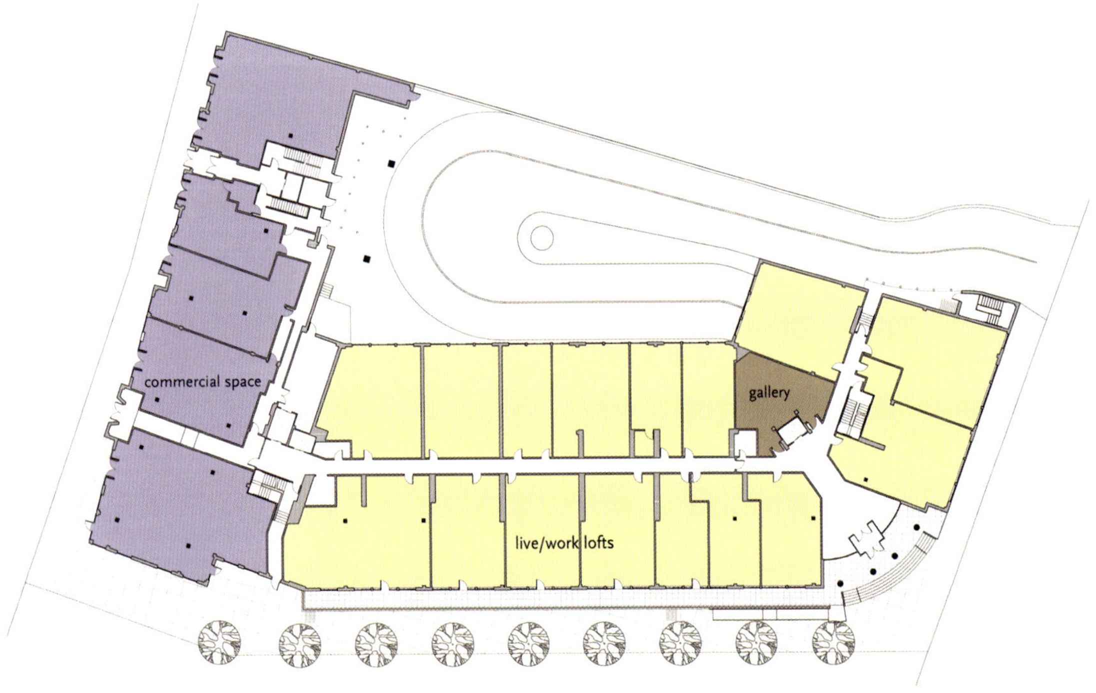

top left Unit interiors are light and open
top right Slender metal railings reinforce industrial flavor
right Different color bricks add scale and variety
opposite top Model of the project's long façade
opposite left Sunlight floods the units even in tight spaces
opposite right The complex's welcoming entrance
Photography Richard Mandlekorn

LACONIA LOFTS

Avenue Lofts

Fort Lauderdale, Florida, USA

Krupnick Studio

Avenue Lofts is the first phase of a large development taking shape in downtown Fort Lauderdale, set amidst a thriving arts center. Just south of the development is the city's art museum, riverwalk, library, and a performing arts center. To the east is Florida Atlantic University and Victoria Park. The condominium project draws its strength from its combination of residential with retail and cultural amenities nearby. Commercial space occupies the ground level, surmounted with three stories of residential lofts and a roof-top with a garden and pool, which will connect to the roof-tops of other buildings in the Avenue Lofts development via catwalks. Seven buildings will eventually make up the development.

The architecture of Avenue Lofts harkens back to the mid-20th century commercial/industrial buildings that pepper the neighborhood around the development site. Materials are left in their raw state: unadorned raw concrete bearing the scars of plywood formwork, steel staircases and pipe railings, corrugated sheet metal, exposed mechanical equipment, and industrial sash windows. Colors are muted. The units have tall windows taking in the surrounding neighborhood, and ceiling heights range from 12 to 20 feet. The aesthetic replicates the best of rehabilitated loft buildings in their casual grittiness. In the case of Avenue Lofts, this sense of architectural understatement is very carefully contrived, giving the project its simultaneous sense of nostalgic and cutting edge design that is ultimately timeless.

More than simply a residential building, this project is a piece of city-making, an essential and connected part of urban fabric that is a pedestrian-oriented neighborhood.

bottom Overview of the complete Avenue Lofts development
opposite Lofts' front façade is light and welcoming

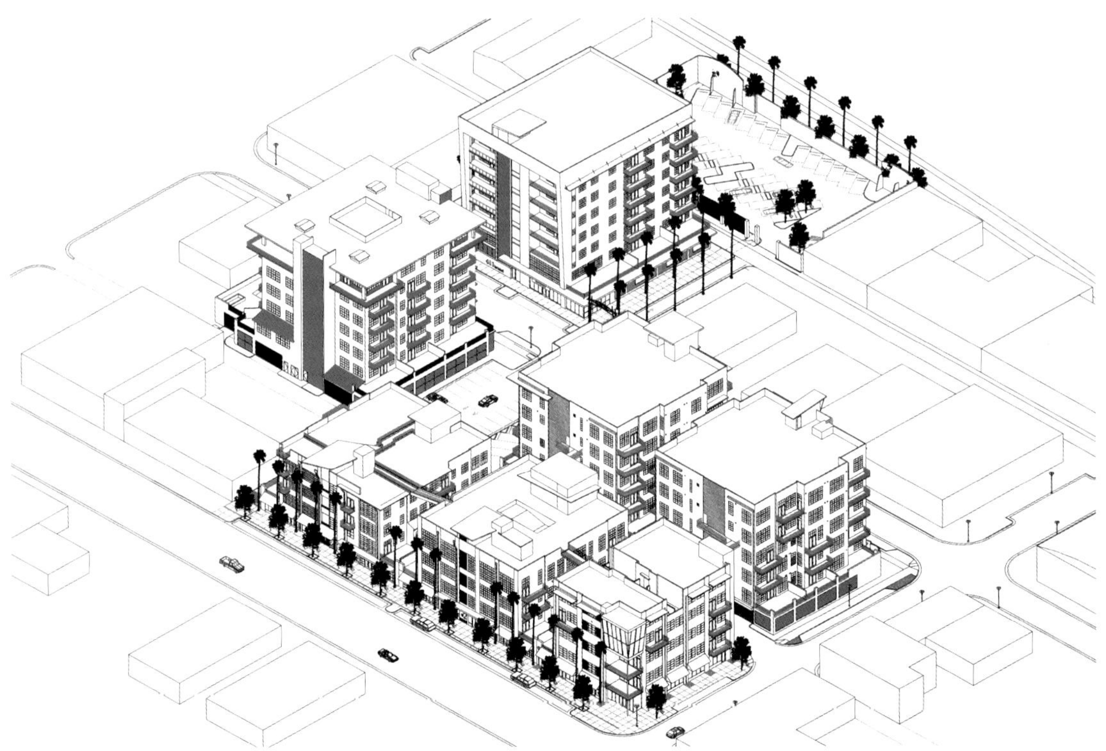

VENUE
OFTS

opposite Materials are left raw in interiors
left Dramatic roof high above the entrance
below Railings are rendered with an industrial aesthetic
bottom Roof plan of complete development, with catwalks

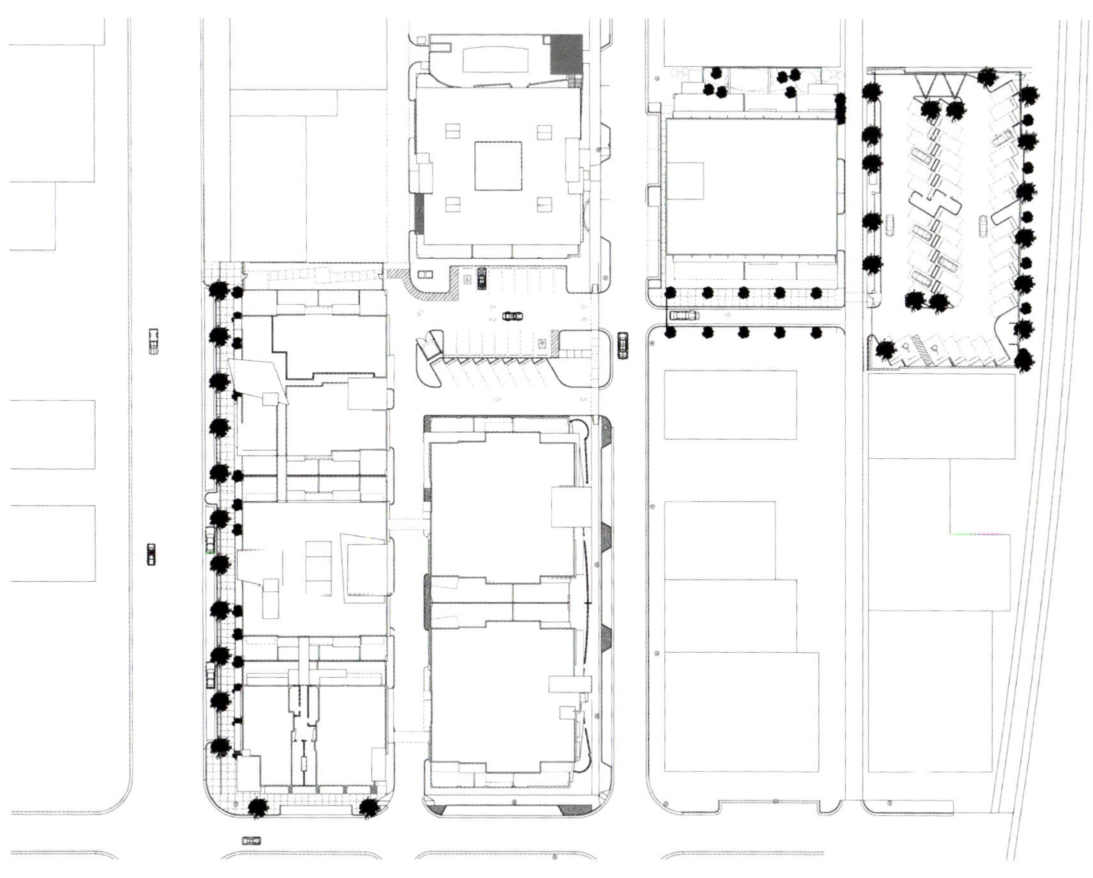

opposite top	Large windows bring the city inside
opposite bottom	Elevation of complete development
top	Kitchen has ample space for art display
Photography	Bill Saunders Photography

Tip Top
Lofts

Toronto, Ontario, Canada

architectsAlliance

The former Tip Top Tailors warehouse is a well-known Toronto landmark. The classic Art Deco structure, designed by Bishop and Miller Architects and completed in 1929, was converted from a disused industrial space into a 252-unit waterfront residential building. Underground parking has been installed in the warehouse basement, supplemented by three levels of below-grade parking, immediately north of the existing building. The ground floor consists of units wrapping the exterior of the building. The interior of the building is comprised of 12,000 square feet of amenity space for residents.

The Tip Top parcel is one of the last sites to be redeveloped on the original Harborfront lands. The renovated and expanded building, sited between the water and Lake Shore Boulevard West, immediately east of the Canadian National Exhibition Grounds, marks the western edge of the Harborfront precinct. Given its location, the building has been a landmark on the Toronto waterfront; the successful redevelopment of the building guarantees that it will remain so for future generations.

The existing five-story, U-shaped building, constructed of reinforced concrete, has been in-filled with a six-story structural steel frame. The addition was deliberately set back from the existing exterior walls and clad primarily in glass to allow a clear reading of the existing historic structure as distinct from the new construction.

Units in the original warehouse have relatively large open floor-plans, which has enabled the client to capitalize on the popularity of loft-style condominiums, and which preserves and highlights the original building structure. Units in the new portion have been designed to maximize natural light and views to the lake and the city.

bottom New glassy addition rises from the masonry original
opposite Top floors addition surmounts Art Deco landmark

TIP TOP TAILORS

TIP TOP TAILORS

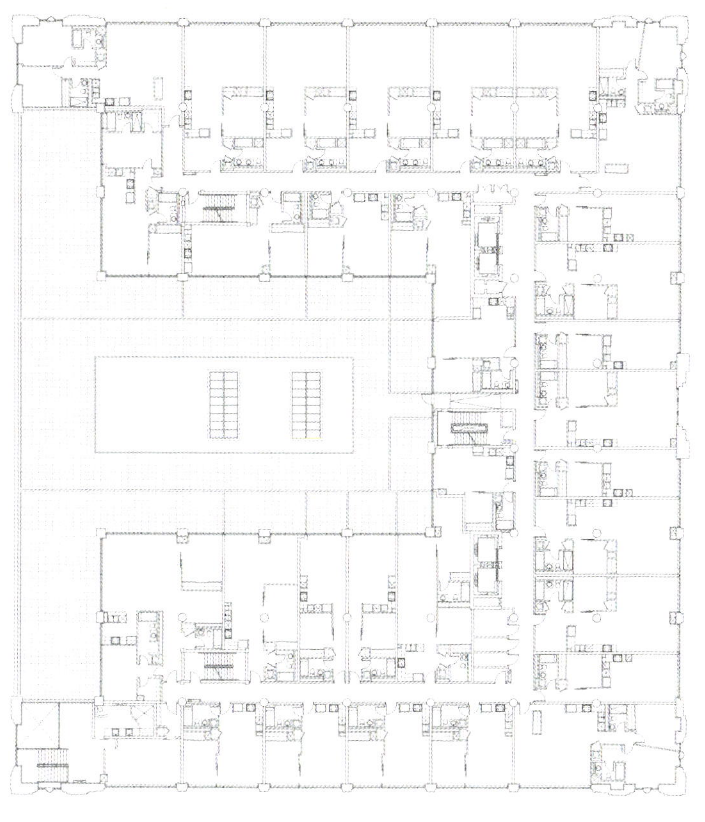

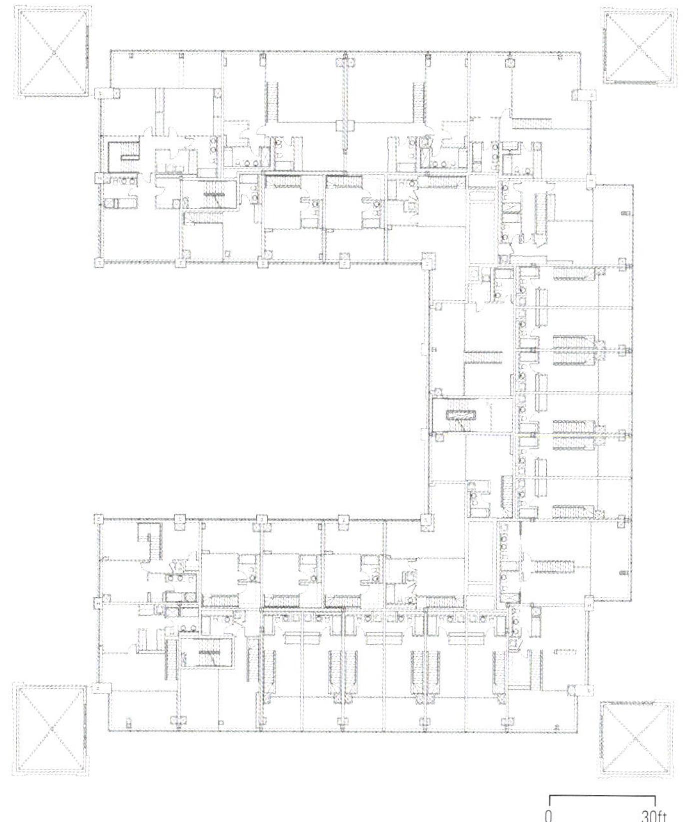

opposite Building's front entry addresses curved drive
top left Plan shows how new units wrap interior amenity space
top right Upper-level plan
bottom left Side wing is topped with new floors
bottom right Art Deco details contrast with new construction
Photography A-Frame/Ben Rahn

Colorado Court

Santa Monica, California, USA

Pugh Scarpa Kodama

top Photovoltaic panels are prominent on front façade
opposite top Site plan of building at corner
opposite bottom Northwest elevation as it faces Colorado Avenue

Colorado Court, which contains 44 single-resident-occupancy units and support spaces, employs a number of energy efficiency strategies that loosens the building's dependence on the electrical utility grid. It distinguishes itself from most conventionally developed projects in that it incorporates energy-efficient measures that exceed standard practice, optimize building performance, and ensure reduced energy use during all phases of construction and occupancy.

The planning and design of Colorado Court emerged from close consideration and employment of passive solar design strategies. These strategies include: locating and orienting the building to control solar cooling loads; shaping and orienting the building for exposure to prevailing winds; shaping the building to induce buoyancy for natural ventilation; designing windows to maximize daylighting; shading south-facing windows and minimizing west-facing glazing; designing windows to maximize natural ventilation; shaping and planning the interior to enhance daylight and natural air flow distribution.

The project features several advanced technologies that distinguish it as a model demonstration building of sustainable energy supply and utilization. A natural-gas-powered turbine/heat recovery system generates the building's base electrical load along with the hot water. A solar photovoltaic panel system integrated into the façade and roof of the building supplies most of the peak-load electricity demand. The co-generation system converts utility natural gas to electricity to meet the base-load power needs of the building and captures waste heat to produce hot water for the building throughout the year as well as space heating needs in the winter. This system has a conversion efficiency of natural gas in excess of 85 percent compared to a less than 30 percent conversion efficiency of primary energy delivered by the utility grid at the building site.

The photovoltaic system produces green electricity at the building site that does not release pollutants into the environment. The panels are integral to the building envelope and unused solar-generated power is delivered to the grid during the daytime and retrieved from the grid at night as needed. These systems will pay for themselves in less than a decade, and annual savings in electricity and natural gas bills are estimated to be in excess of $6000.

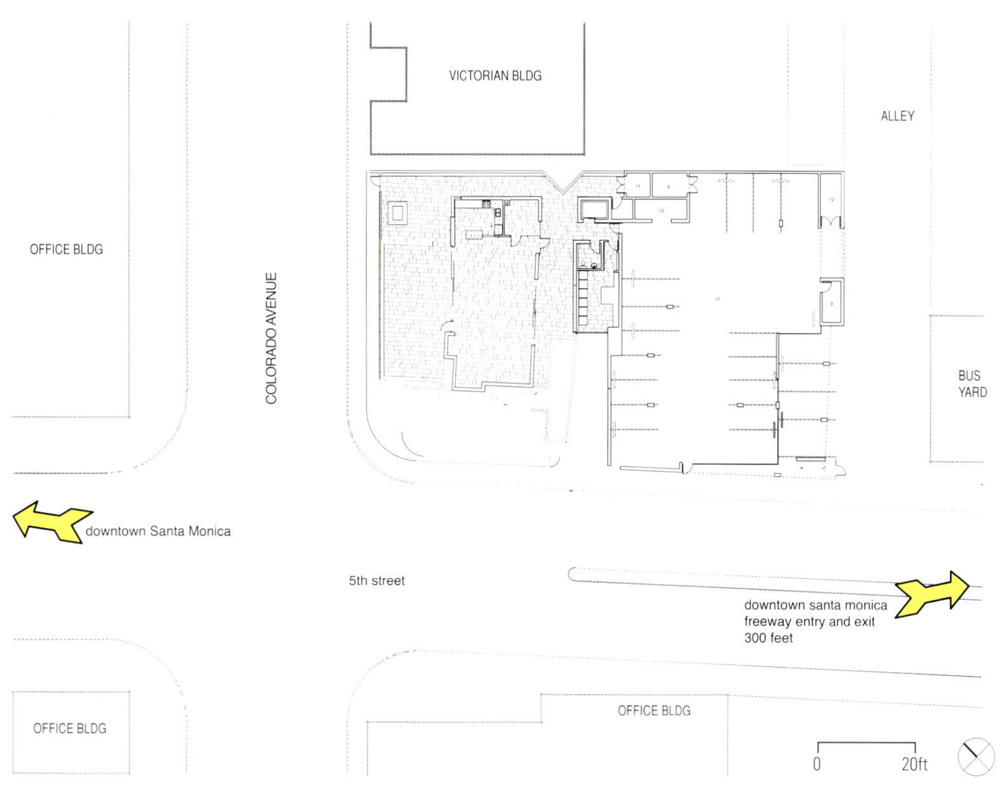
VICTORIAN BLDG
ALLEY
OFFICE BLDG
COLORADO AVENUE
BUS
YARD
downtown Santa Monica
5th street
downtown santa monica
freeway entry and exit
300 feet
OFFICE BLDG
OFFICE BLDG
0
20ft

top	Southwest elevation with photovoltaic panels
above	Exterior circulation weaves through the complex
right	Detail of photovoltaic panels on stair tower
opposite top	Upper-level plan
opposite bottom	Terrace-level plan
opposite right	Panels are integrated with fenestration
Photography	Courtesy of Pugh + Scarpa Architecture

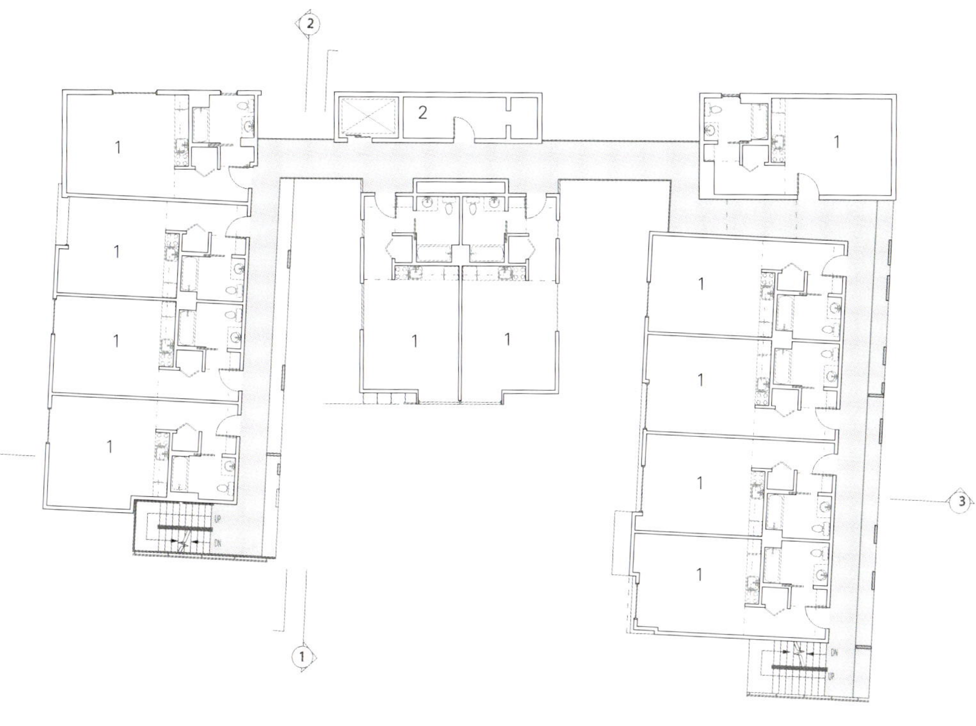

1 Living unit
2 Trash/recycling unit
3 Manager's unit
4 Patio
5 Terrace

Church
Condominiums

Boston, Massachusetts, USA

R. Wendell Phillips and Associates

bottom Church stone exterior was cleaned and repointed
opposite Both the brick rectory and stone church were converted

Saints Peter and Paul Church had not been used for several years when the Roman Catholic Archdiocese of Boston decided to convert it into housing. The neighborhood is part of the expanding Fort Point on west side of South Boston, an area bustling with new residential development. The church dates from 1848 and features three-foot-thick walls made from granite quarried in nearby Quincy.

The design creates 36 units in the church and eight units in an adjacent rectory, with duplexes on the lower level and first floor, two new levels of flats, and penthouse duplexes with outdoor decks cut into the churches slate roof. At the Archdiocese's request, the city policy of 5 percent affordable units was increased to 10 percent.

The granite masonry exterior was restored by cleaning and re-pointing. Existing windows were turned over to the Archdiocese and new casement windows installed. The most difficult and costly part of construction involved slicing into the three-foot-thick granite walls to make new windows. On the rectory the brick masonry was restored by cleaning and re-pointing. New windows match the color and style of the originals. Existing front entrance doors were restored.

The front entry is a glass-walled atrium inside the bell tower which highlights the central multilevel arched window. The condominiums are laid out in a way that preserves the building's wooden columns, arches, trusses, and stained-glass tracery. The interior of every unit features some detailed gem of the original church, along with new amenities such as granite countertops and stainless steel appliances.

Preserving this church and rectory enhances Boston's historic building stock and their adaptive re-use is a sustainable approach to creating needed affordable housing in one of the most expensive real estate markets in the US.

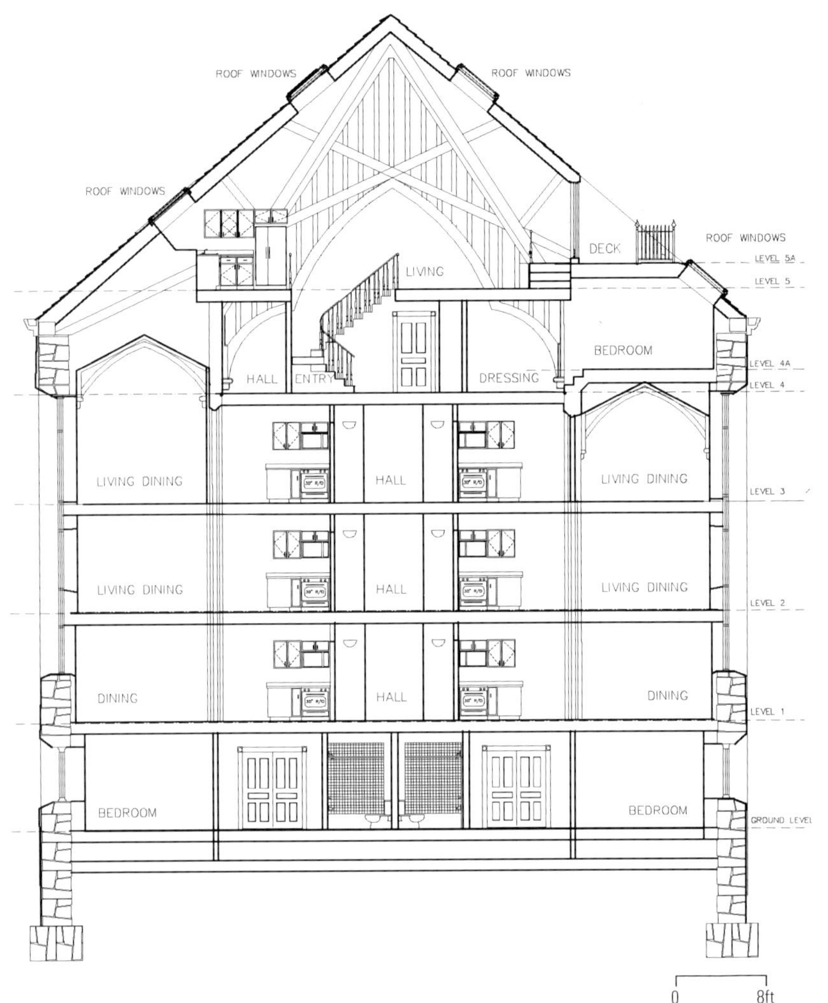

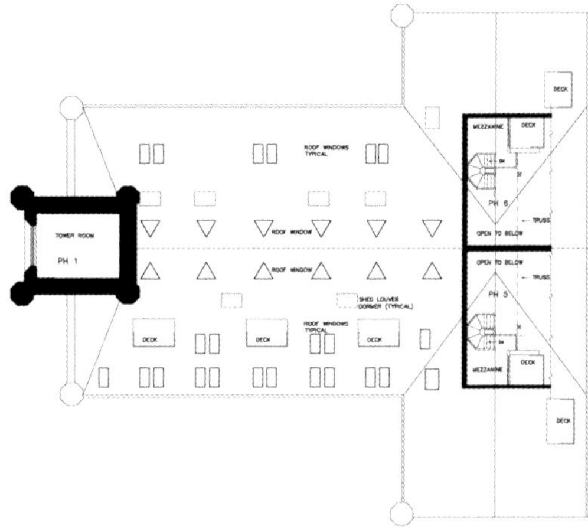

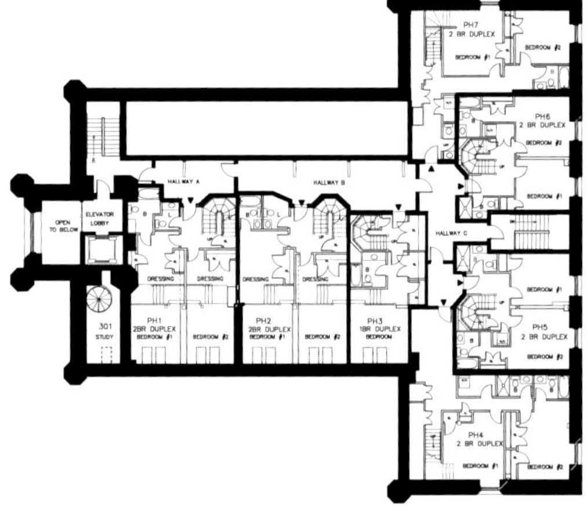

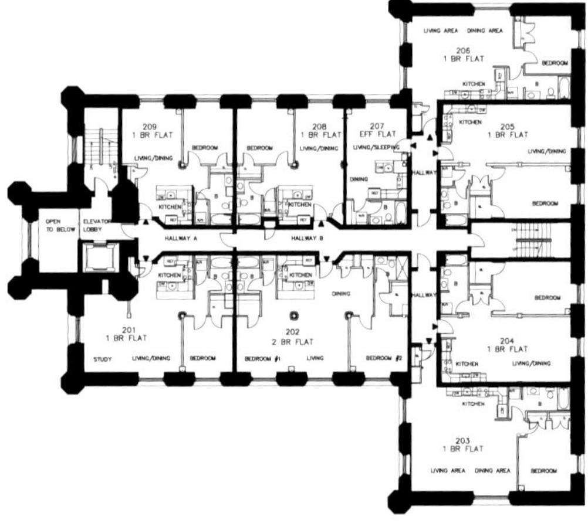

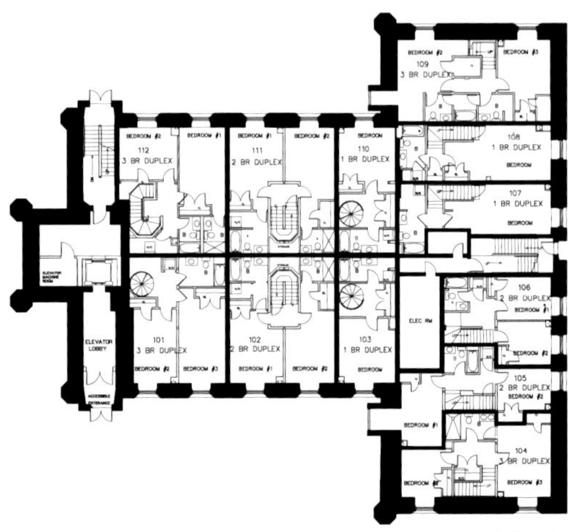

top Section shows how church interior is divided
right Selected floor plans from different levels
opposite Interior detail of top-floor unit

opposite	Existing roof structure is preserved
top	Brick is left exposed, as well as structure
left	Living space in converted rectory unit
Photography	Bob Kramer Photography

Fahrenheit

San Diego, California, USA

Studio E Design

Martinez Cutri (Executive Architect)

The site for Fahrenheit is an L-shaped downtown lot less than a half-acre. The site surrounds a 90-foot-tall parking structure for Petco Park, the downtown ballpark for the San Diego Padres. One leg of the L is only 25 feet deep. The second leg is 60 feet deep. The garage has an access lane across the site.

Seventy-seven units of loft housing are contained in a seven-story structure that conceals the parking garage from the surrounding neighborhood. Parking is located in the basement of this same parking structure and accessed through a below-grade tunnel to the building lobby. Units along the west include ground-level retail spaces in a "shopkeeper" arrangement.

Two types of units respond to the different site conditions. Tall/wide townhouses are placed on the north face of the garage where only 25 feet of site depth restricted access. Deep, single-story lofts line the west edge. The townhouses address the street façade with a weaving of large glazed openings and orange corrugated siding. Balconies and bay windows hang over the right-of-way to increase the depth of the space and afford long east/west views down the San Diego gridiron. The flats, in contrast, are composed in a modulated façade with deep recesses for room-sized outdoor living spaces to take best advantage of the benign San Diego climate. The façade is almost entirely glazed to allow for penetration of light into these deep units.

The cast-in-place concrete structural frame is celebrated and expressed. This open frame is in-filled with storefront glazing and wall panels with corrugated metal sidings making a clear distinction between panel and frame. The north façade's siding is a deep orange color to add "daylight" on a portion of the building that rarely receives direct light. Further, the warm color is intended to complement the historic brick structures nearby.

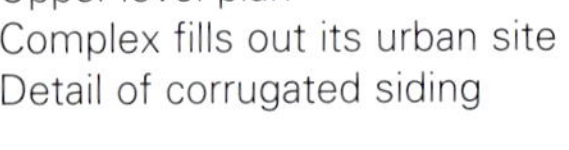

bottom Upper-level plan
opposite top Complex fills out its urban site
opposite bottom Detail of corrugated siding

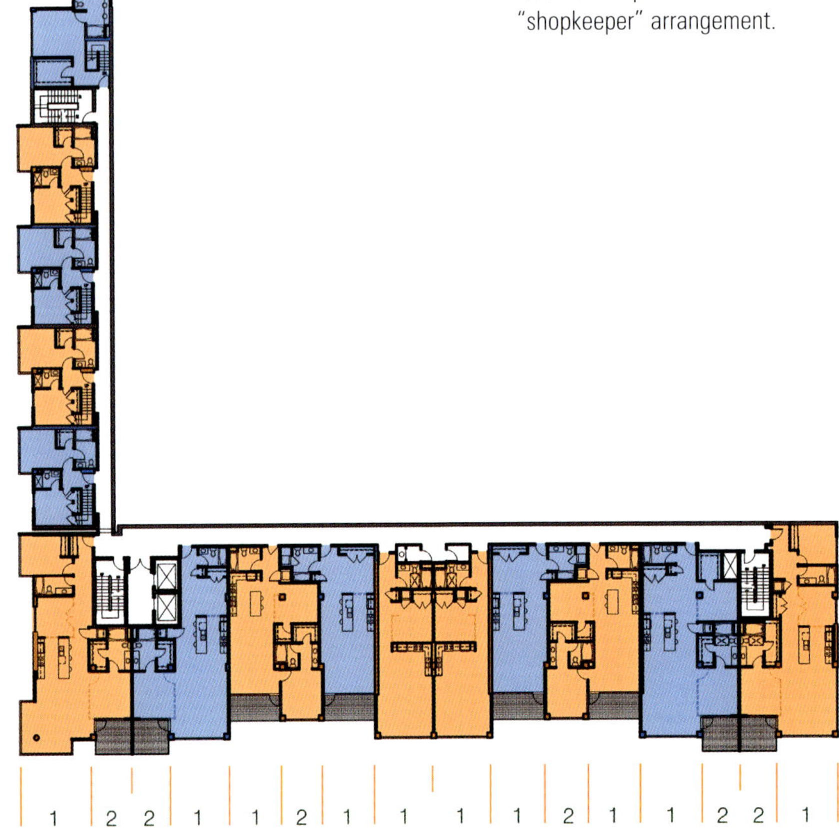

top	Color is used to add character
top right	Retail areas are at street level
bottom	Site plan shows how building wraps parking garage
opposite top left	Parking garage is concealed behind residences
opposite top right	Sliver of narrow building abuts garage
opposite bottom	Island Avenue elevation
Photography	Citymark

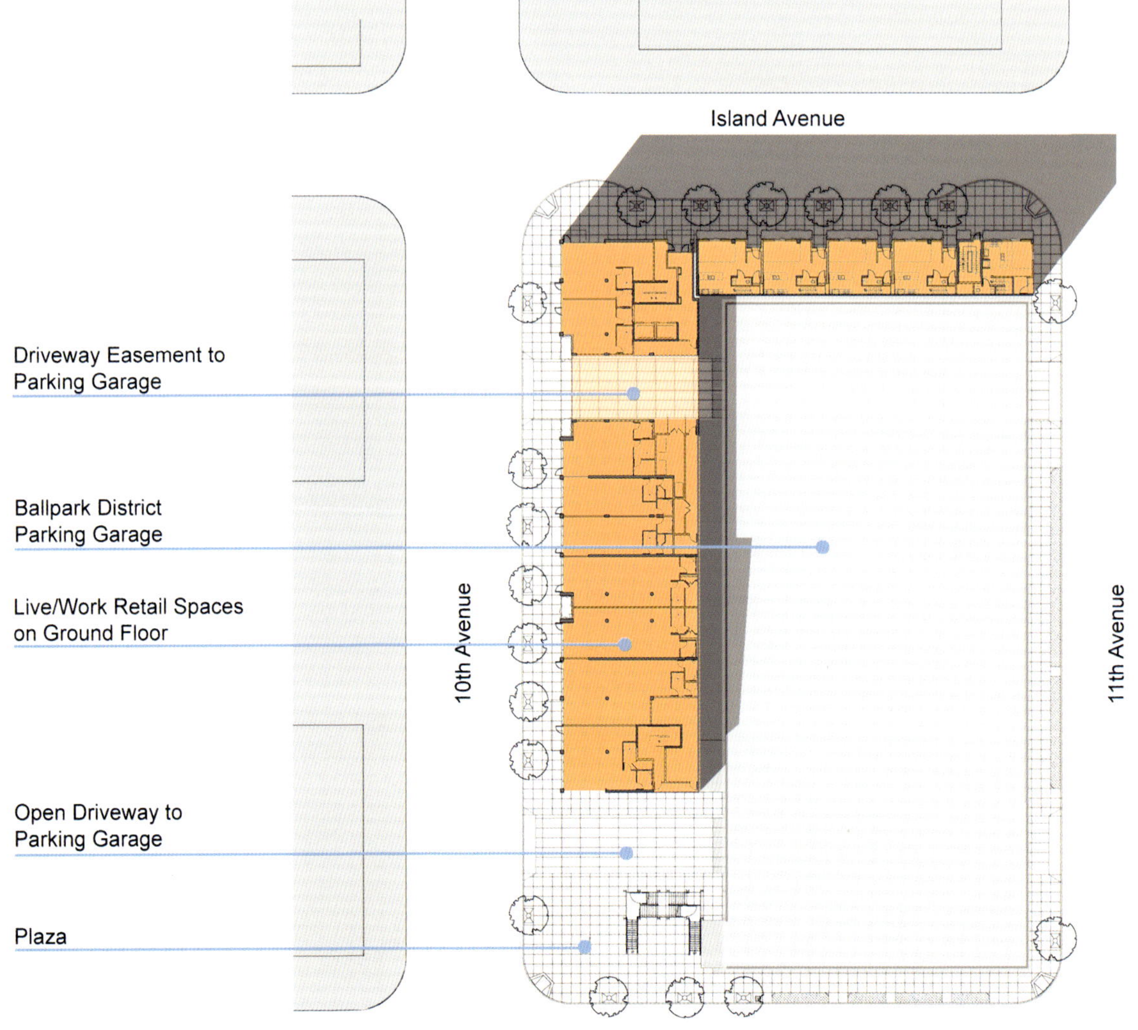

°Fahrenheit

Index of Architects

architectsAlliance 40, 112, 204
www.architectsalliance.com

CBT Architects 138
www.cbtarchitects.com

David Baker + Partners 50, 86, 116, 168
www.dbarchitect.com

David Forbes Hibbert, Architect 34
dfhibbert@earthlink.net

Donna Kacmar, Christopher Craig, Mary Ann Young 172
www.architectworks.com

Fletcher Farr Ayotte and Kevin Cavanaugh 164
www.ffadesign.com

Hacin + Associates 194
www.hacin.com

Harley Ellis Devereaux 126
www.harleyellis.com

Humphries Poli Architects 68, 184
www.hparch.com

Jonathan Segal, Architect 146
www.jonathansegalarchitect.com

Kanner Architects 10, 106
www.kannerarch.com

Koning Eizenberg Architecture 64, 96
www.kearch.com

Krupnick Studio 198
www.krupnickstudio.com

McIntosh Poris Associates 58
www.mcintoshporis.com

Pelli Clarke Pelli 30
www.cesar-pelli.com

Perkins + Will 16
www.perkinswill.com

Pugh + Scarpa Architecture 24, 74, 208
www.pugh-scarpa.com

R. Wendell Phillips and Associates 212
rwpaarch@tds.net

Randy Brown Architects 90
www.randybrownarchitects.com

Robertson, Merryman, Barnes Architects 104
www.rmbarch.com

Ron Wommack Architect 152
www.ronwommack.com

Seidel Holzman 46, 122, 176
www.seidelholzman.com

Steven Ehrlich Architects 132
www.s-ehrlich.com

Studio E Architects 158, 188, 218
www.studioearchitects.com

William Wilson Architects 80
www.wilsonarch.com

Wolff Lyon Architects 56, 118
www.wlarch.com

Acknowledgments

Many people were involved in the creation of this book. Thanks are extended to the architects and designers who agreed to have their projects published. Special gratitude is expressed to the photographers who generously allowed use of their photographs. To my colleagues and friends, I express my thanks for suggesting multi-family projects to include in this book. Particularly, I appreciate the efforts of Julie Taylor and Dianne Ludman Frank. I also want to thank Alessina Brooks and Paul Latham of The Images Publishing Group for their support, encouragement, and friendship, and the staff at IMAGES, especially to my editor, Andrea Boekel, for helping to guide this book to completion.